Medieval Music

The Oxford Anthology of Music

Medieval Music

Edited by W Thomas Marrocco and Nicholas Sandon

Oxford University Press

Music Department   44 Conduit Street, London W1
200 Madison Avenue, New York

For our wives, Audrey and Virginia

© Oxford University Press 1977
First published 1977
ISBN 0 19 323207 3

Printed in Great Britain

Contents

The Ars Antiqua

The Ars Nova

The Fifteenth Century

Introduction

This anthology has been designed for the student, teacher, scholar, and performer alike. It was the intention of the editors to provide a much greater variety of medieval music than had hitherto been attempted. Faithful to the meaning of the term 'anthology' – a garland of flowers – the editors have endeavoured to bring within these pages compositions of artistic and historical significance from a period of nearly a thousand years. They were often embarrassed by the richness of the repertories from which a choice had to be made, but have attempted to provide examples of every important functional, technical, and stylistic aspect of Western art-music (as opposed to folk music) between about AD 600 and 1450. As far as it lay within their power they have avoided duplication with other anthologies and non-specialist publications. Whenever possible they prepared new editions from films or facsimiles of the sources or from the sources themselves. In the dozen-or-so cases in which a music example was taken from an existing edition, due acknowledgement has been made in the commentary. Except in the case of cyclic masses, when for reasons of space only a single movement from each cycle could be printed, the policy has been to include only complete compositions. The commentaries are intended to place each extract in its context and to call attention to its most important technical and stylistic features. They also include full translations of the text, except for the spoken items in Examples 10 and 11.

In spite of checking and re-checking there will be errors in this anthology – misstatements of fact, ill-founded comments, questionable interpretations of the sources, inconsistencies, unnoticed mis-copyings, uncorrected misprints, etc. The editors would be grateful to have these pointed out to them, together with suggestions of other ways in which the anthology might be improved.

Musical texts
In all except the plainsong items the original clef, mensuration sign, and first note-symbol of each voice is given, followed by the clef used in the transcription and an indication of the voice's compass. Original note values have been reduced sixteenfold or eightfold in music written before about 1290; thereafter fourfold reduction (brevis = quarter-note) has usually been employed. No attempt has been made to produce rhythmic versions of plainsong compositions, of polyphonic items dating from before the Notre Dame period, or of the more melodically elaborate examples of secular monophony. No one is in a position to be dogmatic about the rhythmic interpretation of music written much before 1200; rather than give a false impression of certainty where none exists, the editors have adopted non-rhythmic transcription for pieces whose rhythmic character seems particularly debatable.

A great deal of medieval polyphony formed part of the liturgy; it set only part of a text, the rest of which was sung in plainsong. In such instances the relevant portions of plainchant have been supplied editorially.

The editors have not hesitated to emend manuscript readings which, in the light of modern understanding of the style concerned, cannot have represented the composer's intention. In these cases the reading of the main source is given in a footnote. It was obviously impractical to print a detailed collation of all the sources of every composition.

For most of the period covered by this anthology monophonic and polyphonic music was 'edited' in performance by inflecting certain notes – by making them sharp, flat, or natural – where the source did not indicate such alteration. A medieval musician was expected and trained to do this, and failure to do so makes for an unstylish, if not exactly 'incorrect' performance. Unfortunately, the premises governing the application of these inflections, generally known as 'musica ficta', were stated rather imprecisely by medieval theorists, and were in any case liable to change from time to time and place to place. The editors have added *musica ficta* accidentals above the stave according to what they conceive to have been the conventions operating at the time and place of a composition's origin. They are well aware that in so doing they place their heads on a musicological chopping-block, but hope to stay the descent of the critical axe by invoking, as did medieval theorists, the magic formula 'causa pulchritudinis'.

Verbal texts
Where a standard modern edition of a text was available, it has been used and the fact acknowledged in the commentary. Other Latin texts have been modernized in spelling, capitalization, and punctuation following the style of the *Liber Usualis*. Texts in other languages have been printed as they appear in the main source. The translations are by various hands. The editors are grateful to the following for their help in preparing and revising translations: their colleagues at the Universities of Exeter and California; Betty Rahv (Boston College); J. W. Thomas (University of Kentucky); Barbara Reynolds and Lewis Thorpe (University of Nottingham); T. Newcombe (University of Edinburgh); Lewis Jillings (University of Stirling); and G. B. Gybbon-Monypenny (University of Manchester).

The commentaries
Musical sources are listed first. For monophonic items the main source only is listed; for polyphonic items the main source is followed by the others. RISM sigla are used where possible. If a printed version of the text and/or a printed translation have been used, this is listed next. The analysis and comment follow, after which comes the translation.

Some notes on performance
This anthology is intended to have a practical use as well as an academic one. We hope that its users will attempt to bring the music to life in performance, and with this in mind we make the following suggestions, which are general in their application.

1. Examples may be transposed to any suitable pitch. There was no standard pitch in the Middle Ages, and we have reproduced the written pitch only for the sake of consistency.

2. We have used bar-lines in order to make some examples easier to read. They do not necessarily indicate regularly-occurring strong and weak beats, as the bar-lines in more modern music tend to do. Bar-lines practically never occur in medieval music, and the modern performer must be on his guard not to let those in an edition interfere with the

integrity of each individual melodic line.

3. Examples 1–43 and 51–54 may be performed with a considerable amount of rhythmic freedom. The accentuation of the text and the contour of the melody should act as a guide for the examples in plainsong notation. We do not claim infallibility where we have provided a rhythmic interpretation of these examples; the informed reader may wish to adjust note values or to alter the length of rests.

4. The informed reader is likewise at liberty to substitute his own editorial accidentals in place of ours.

5. Tempi are left to the discretion of the performer. They should probably be lively rather than funereal, so long as clear enunciation and articulation remain possible.

6. Instrumental participation is in order (except probably for Examples 1–11 and 37–42). Instruments may double or replace voices on texted lines, or play parts which do not have text. Untexted parts may also be vocalized to a single vowel sound, or sung to solmization syllables. The addition of percussion to dances and secular songs is often effective.

Symbols

1. In plainsong, ligatures are shown thus:

2. In polyphony, ligatures are shown thus (but see 3.):

3. In polyphony and secular monophony the ligature known as the conjunctura is shown by this symbol over the diamond-shaped notes:

4. In polyphony and secular monophony, the plica is shown by a note with a diagonal stroke through its stem, thus:

5. In plainsong, the last note in a liquescent neume is printed smaller than the other notes.

6. In plainsong, a quilisma is shown thus:

7. In polyphony, coloration is shown thus:

8. Manuscript accidentals are printed on the stave immediately before the note to which the editors have taken them to apply. Editorial accidentals are printed above the stave, over the appropriate note. Both types of accidental apply to all repetitions of the relevant pitch in the bar in which they appear.

9. Small notes and italic text have been added editorially.

Isorhythmic compositions

1. Statements of the same *color* are shown by A^1, A^2, A^3 . . .

2. Statements of a second *color* are shown by B^1, B^2, B^3 . . .

3. Statements of a first *talea* are shown by I, II, III . . .

4. Statements of a second *talea* are shown by 1, 2, 3 . . .

5. The fractions $x\frac{2}{3}$, $x\frac{1}{2}$, $x\frac{1}{3}$ indicate the statement of a *talea* in note values reduced by one third, one half, and two thirds respectively.

6. R indicates the statement of a *talea* or *color* in retrograde.

Abbreviations

AS W. H. Frere, *Antiphonale Sarisburiense* (London, 1901–25).

GS W. H. Frere, *Graduale Sarisburiense* (London, 1894).

LU *Liber Usualis* (Tournai, 1961).

R   G. Raynaud, *Bibliographie des Chansonniers Français des XIIIe et XIVe siècles* (Paris, 1884)

US W. H. Frere, *The Use of Sarum* (Cambridge, 1898–1901)

Bibliography

F. W. Sternfeld, ed., *A History of Western Music,* Vol. I (London, 1973).

The New Oxford History of Music, Vols. II and III (London, 1954 and 1960).

These excellent volumes have comprehensive bibliographies which it would be pointless to duplicate. Complete or collected editions which contain editions of our examples are cited in a separate list (see p. 240).

Sacred Monophony

1. He parthenos semeron

Kontakion of Romanos for Christmas Day (Byzantine, 6th century)

E. Wellesz, *A History of Byzantine Music and Hymnography* (Oxford, 1961), pp. 401–3.

The Byzantine chant repertory evolved between the 4th and 15th centuries to satisfy the liturgical requirements of the Greek Orthodox church and the ceremonial needs of its imperial sponsors. Much of it consisted of hymnography cast in the form of the Kontakion – a poetic sermon consisting of a number of similarly constructed stanzas or Troparia (singular Troparion) – or of the Kanon – a sequence of nine hymns of praise or Odai. The Kontakia seem to have originated early in the 6th century and were to some extent influenced by Syriac poetry; they were overtaken in popularity by the Kanons late in the 7th century. Active at Constantinople during the reign of Anastasios I (491–518), Romanos was regarded as the greatest writer of Kontakia. Wellesz points out that in both the Kontakion and the Kanon 'music and poetry had to make a single entity' and that their composition 'was a task which a poet could not achieve who was not also a skilled musician'. The connection between the form of the text and the repetition of melodic phrases will be evident in this example. The reader will also notice that Byzantine notation differed from its Gregorian counterpart in that it evolved a method of notating rhythm and included symbols for phrasing and interpretation. The syllables 'anan, ananes' indicate intonation formulae.

TRANSLATION
The Virgin today gives birth to the Almighty; and the earth leads the heavens towards the unapproachable. Angels and shepherds praise him; the magi with the star journey towards him. For our sake he was born, the young child, the God before ages.

2. Crux fidelis *and* Pange lingua

Refrain and Hymn for feasts of the Holy Cross (Gallican, late 6th century)

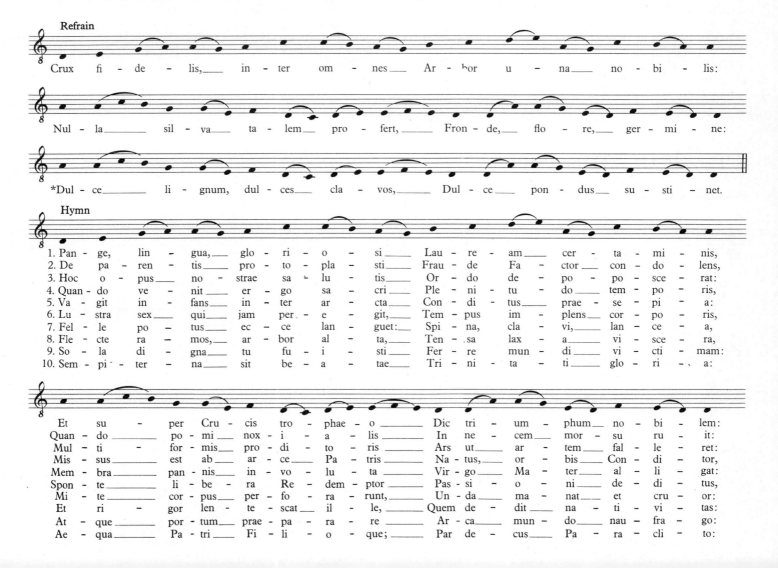

Qua - li - - - ter Re - dem - ptor - or - bis _____ Im - mo - la - tus vi - ce - rit.
Ip - se _____ li - gnum_ tunc no - ta - vit, _____ Dam - na - li - gni ut sol - ve - ret.
Et me - - - de - lam fer - ret in - de, _____ Ho - stis_ un - de lae - se - rat.
At - que _____ ven - tre - vir - gi - na - li _____ Car - ne a - mi - ctus pro - di - it.
Et De - - i ma - nus pe - des - que _____ Stri - cta_ cin - git fa - sci - a.
A - gnus _____ in Cru - cis le - va - tur _____ Im - mo - lan - dus_ sti - pi - te.
Ter - ra, _____ pon - tus, _____ a - stra, _____ mun - dus, _____ Quo la - van - tur_ flu - mi - ne!
Et su - - per - ni_mem - bra Re - gis Ten - de - mi - ti sti - pi - te.
Quam sa - - cer cru - or per - un - xit, _____ Fu - sus_ A - gni cor - po - re.
U - ni - - us Tri - ni - que_ no - men Lau - det_ u - ni - ver - si - tas.

The first four lines of the refrain are sung after every odd-numbered verse and the last two lines of the refrain are sung after every even-numbered verse. At the end of the last verse is sung

A - men._

LU, pp. 742–5.
Translation from *Hymns Ancient and Modern,* no. 97.

The Gallican liturgy and its chant were in use in the Frankish kingdoms between about 400 and 800, when it was supplanted by the Roman rite. It seems to have been related more closely to the Mozarabic and Ambrosian liturgies than to that of Rome, although the scarcity of indisputably Gallican melodies inhibits detailed comparison. *Crux fidelis* and *Pange lingua* (the latter by Venantius Fortunatus, died *c*.600) were items from the Office on feasts of the Holy Cross which the Roman church adopted and transferred to the afternoon liturgy on Good Friday.

TRANSLATION

Faithful Cross, above all other, One and only noble Tree, None in foliage, none in blossom, None in fruit thy peer may be; Sweetest wood, and sweetest iron; Sweetest weight is hung on thee.

Sing, my tongue, the glorious battle, Sing the last, the dread affray; O'er the Cross, the Victor's trophy, Sound the high triumphal lay, How, the pains of death enduring, Earth's Redeemer won the day.

He, our Maker, deeply grieving That the first-made Adam fell, When he ate the fruit forbidden Whose reward was death and hell, Marked e'en then this Tree the ruin Of the first tree to dispel.

Thus the work for our salvation He ordained to be done; To the traitor's art opposing Art yet deeper than his own; Thence the remedy procuring Whence the fatal wound begun. Therefore, when at length the fulness of the appointed time was come, He was sent, the world's Creator, From the Father's heavenly home, And was found in human fashion, Offspring of the Virgin's womb.

Lo! He lies, an Infant weeping, Where the narrow manger stands, While the Mother-Maid His members Wraps in mean and lowly bands, And the swaddling clothes is winding Round His helpless Feet and Hands.

Now the thirty years accomplished Which on earth He willed to see, Born for this, He meets His Passion, Gives Himself an offering free; On the Cross the Lamb is lifted, There the Sacrifice to be.

There the nails and spear He suffers, Vinegar, and gall, and reed; From His sacred Body pierced Blood and Water both proceed; Precious blood, which all creation From the stain of sin hath freed.

Bend, O lofty Tree, thy branches, Thy too rigid sinews bend; And awhile the stubborn hardness, Which thy birth bestowed, suspend; And the Limbs of Heaven's high Monarch Gently on thine arms extend.

Thou alone wast counted worthy This world's ransome to sustain, That a shipwrecked race for ever Might a port of refuge gain, With the sacred Blood anointed Of the Lamb for sinners slain. Praise and honour to the Father, Praise and honour to the Son, praise and honour to the Spirit, Ever Three and ever One, One in might, and One in glory, While eternal ages run.

3a. Deus miserere

Prece from Office for the dead   (Mozarabic)

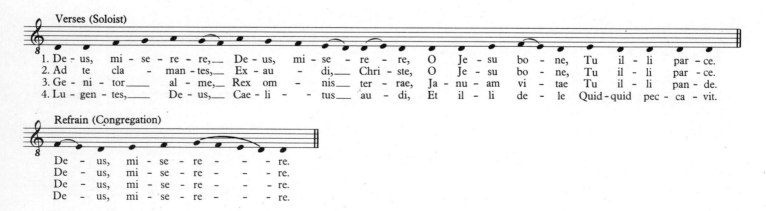

Verses (Soloist)

1. De - us, mi - se - re - re, _____ De - us, mi - se - re - re, O Je - su bo - ne, Tu il - li par - ce.
2. Ad te cla - man - tes, _____ Ex - au - di, Chri - ste, O Je - su bo - ne, Tu il - li par - ce.
3. Ge - ni - tor _____ al - me, Rex om - nis - ter - rae, Ja - nu - am vi - tae Tu il - li pan - de.
4. Lu - gen - tes, _____ De - us, _____ Cae - li - tus _____ au - di, Et il - li de - le Quid - quid pec - ca - vit.

Refrain (Congregation)

De - us, mi - se - re - - - re.
De - us, mi - se - re - - - re.
De - us, mi - se - re - - - re.
De - us, mi - se - re - - - re.

3b. Si ascendero

Antiphon from Office for the dead   (Mozarabic)

G. Prado, 'Mozarabic Melodies' in *Speculum*, III (1928), pp. 235 and 237.

The Mozarabic liturgy developed in Spain during the Visigothic period and continued to be used by the Christian populace during the Moorish occupation. After the Christian reconquest of the country, however, it was gradually replaced by the Roman rite, although vestiges survived on a purely local basis. Few Mozarabic melodies have been preserved in notation whose pitch is unequivocal. Some of those which have done so resemble Ambrosian plainsong, and there are similarities between the two liturgies. *Deus miserere* is a simple chant consisting of solo verses and a congregational refrain, while *Si ascendero* is a more elaborate setting of psalmody.

TRANSLATION

3a: Lord, have mercy; Lord, have mercy; O, good Jesus, have pity for him. Lord, have mercy.

Hear, O Christ, those calling to thee; O, good Jesus, have pity for him. Lord, have mercy.

Kind begetter, king of all the earth, entrance to life, reach out for him. Lord, have mercy.

Hear us mourning, heavenly God, and wipe out his sins for him. Lord, have mercy.

3b: If I ascend up into heaven, Thou art there: if I make my bed in hell, behold, Thou art there. Reach out Thine hand, O Lord; deliver me from lower hell.

4. A summo caelo

Psalmellus from Mass for the second Sunday in Advent   (Ambrosian)

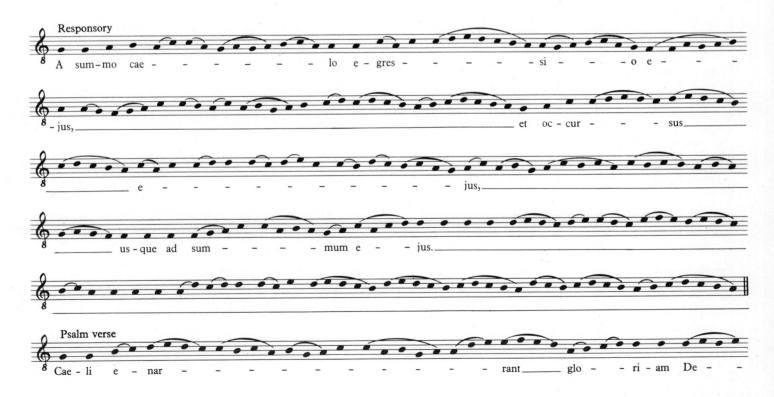

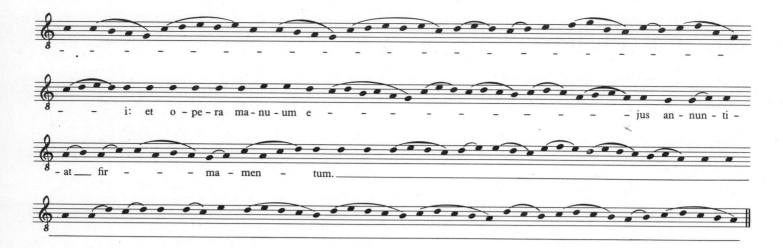

London, British Library, MS Add. 34209, f. 4r.

The Ambrosian liturgy resisted Roman encroachment more effectively than did the Gallican and Mozarabic rites, surviving in much of northern Italy until the 14th century and being still in use in Milan and some neighbouring areas. The chant takes its name from St Ambrose, who was Bishop of Milan between 374 and 397, but none of its constituents is known to have such an ancient origin. Despite the cross-fertilization which occurred between the Ambrosian and Gregorian repertories, Ambrosian plainsong shows more evidence than does Gregorian plainsong of its early melodic characteristics; these include signs of

Syrian and Greek influence as well as unusual turns of melody, all of which may have been edited out of the Roman liturgy by the Gregorian reformers. Melismatic Ambrosian chants, such as the Psalmellus (Gradual), are often more elaborate than their Gregorian counterparts; comparison of *A summo caeli* with the Gregorian version (LU, pp. 343–4) will demonstrate this.

TRANSLATION
It goeth forth from the uttermost part of the heaven, and runneth about unto the end of it again. The heavens declare the glory of God: and the firmament sheweth His handy-work.

5. Gregorian plainsong modes

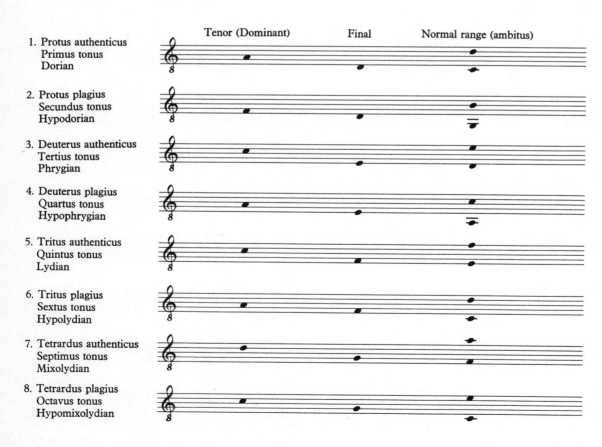

	Tenor (Dominant)	Final	Normal range (ambitus)
1. Protus authenticus Primus tonus Dorian			
2. Protus plagius Secundus tonus Hypodorian			
3. Deuterus authenticus Tertius tonus Phrygian			
4. Deuterus plagius Quartus tonus Hypophrygian			
5. Tritus authenticus Quintus tonus Lydian			
6. Tritus plagius Sextus tonus Hypolydian			
7. Tetrardus authenticus Septimus tonus Mixolydian			
8. Tetrardus plagius Octavus tonus Hypomixolydian			

Odo of Cluny (*d*.942), 'Dialogus de Musica' in M. Gerbert, *Scriptores Ecclesiastici de Musica* . . . (St Blaise, 1784), I, pp. 259–64.

The Gregorian modal system was assembled between the 7th and 9th centuries, partly on Byzantine models, partly on an inadequate understanding of classical Greek music theory and partly through study of plainchant melodies. Its function was to make possible the classification of the existing plainsong repertory rather than to provide a theoretical basis for new composition. The codification was based on the criteria of range, final note, and certain commonly-occurring melodic formulae. The resulting modes embodied these qualities rather than being scales in the modern sense. Each of the four modes existed in two forms – an authentic form and a plagal form which was lower in range but which had the same final (i.e. note on which the melodies in that mode ended). The *tenor* or *dominant* (also known as *tuba*), not actually referred to by Odo, was a note second in importance to the final, frequently used as a point of reference or repose in the middle of a plainsong; the term 'dominant' has no harmonic significance. The modal system existed to codify plainsong; its application to other types of monophonic music and to the polyphonic repertory is of questionable value and was in dispute among medieval theorists themselves.

6. *Psalm* Beatus vir *with antiphon* Erat autem aspectus *to the eighth psalm tone*

Third psalm at Vespers on Easter Day (Gregorian)

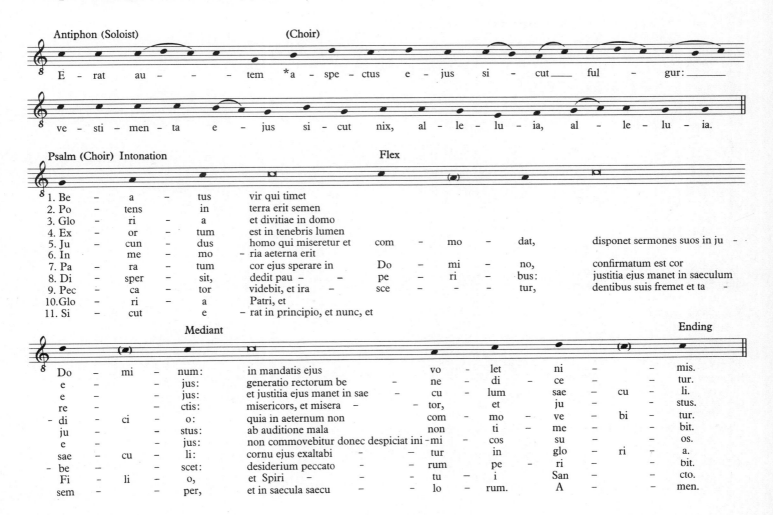

The antiphon is repeated after the *Gloria Patri*.
LU, pp. 147 and 782.

The worship of the Western church took two forms – the Mass, or celebration of the Lord's Supper, and the Daily Office. The services of the latter, namely Matins, Lauds, Prime, Terce, Sext, None, Vespers, and Compline, were centred around the singing of psalms. A psalm was sung with an *antiphon* – a short biblical text selected to emphasize the relevance of the psalm to a particular occasion. Usually only the opening phrase of the antiphon was sung before the psalm; then the entire psalm and the

Gloria Patri (*doxology*) were sung *alternatim* – i.e. with the two sides of the choir singing alternate verses – after which the choir sang the complete antiphon. A psalm was sung to a *psalm tone* – basically, a recitation on a monotone with a decorated *intonation* (beginning), *mediant* (mid-way cadence) and *ending* (final cadence); the *flex* was an inflexion between the intonation and the mediant and was used only when the psalm verse was unusually long. There was one psalm tone in each of the modes.
TRANSLATION
Indeed, His appearance was like lightning: His garments like snow, alleluia, alleluia.

Blessed is the man that feareth the Lord: he hath great delight in His commandments.

His seed shall be mighty upon earth: the generation of the faithful shall be blessed.

Riches and plenteousness shall be in his house: and his righteousness endureth for ever.

Unto the godly there ariseth up light in the darkness: he is merciful, loving, and righteous.

A good man is merciful, and lendeth, and will guide his words with discretion: for he shall never be moved.

The righteous shall be had in everlasting remembrance: he will not be afraid of any evil tidings.

His heart standeth fast, and believeth in the Lord; his heart is established: and will not shrink, until he see his desire upon his enemies.

He hath dispersed abroad, and given to the poor: and his righteousness remaineth for ever: his horn shall be exalted with honour.

The ungodly shall see it, and it shall grieve him, he shall gnash his teeth and consume away: the desire of the ungodly shall perish.

Glory be to the Father, and to the Son: and to the Holy Ghost.

As it was in the beginning, is now, and ever shall be: world without end. Amen.

7. *Psalm* In exitu Israel, *with antiphon* Deus autem noster, *to the tonus peregrinus*

Fifth psalm at Vespers on Sundays (Gregorian)

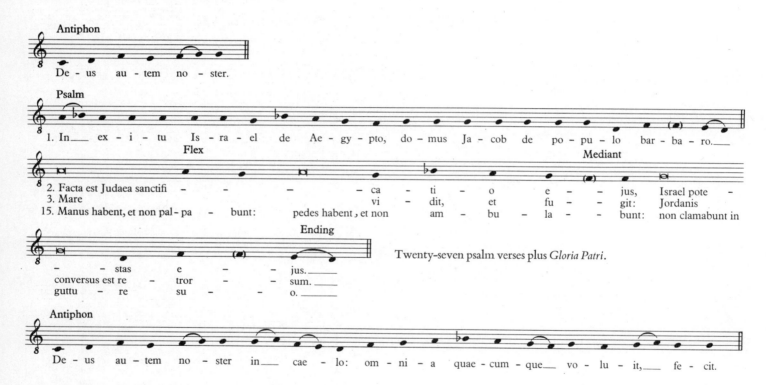

Twenty-seven psalm verses plus *Gloria Patri*.

During Eastertide this Alleluia is sung after the complete antiphon:

LU, pp. 254–6.

The psalm *In exitu Israel* was sung to a special psalm tone which stood outside the modal system and was called the *tonus peregrinus*. This tone was used for no other text and was exceptional in having different reciting notes for each half of the verses.

TRANSLATION

Our God is even in heaven: whatsoever He has wished, He has made. Alleluia.

When Israel came out of Egypt, and the house of Jacob from among the strange people.

Judah was his sanctuary, and Israel his dominion.

The sea saw that, and fled: Jordan was driven back.

They have hands, and handle not: feet have they, and walk not: neither speak they through their throat.

8. *Responsory* Hodie nobis caelorum Rex

First responsory at Matins on Christmas Day **(Gregorian)**

Responsory (Soloists)   (Choir)

Ho - di - - e *no - bis_____ cae - lo - rum Rex_____ de Vir - - gi - ne

na - - - sci di - - - - - gna - tus_____ est,__ ut__ ho - mi -

- nem_____ per - di - tum___ ad__ cae - le - - - - - sti - a re - - -

- - gna re - - vo - - - - ca - - - ret:__ Gau - - det ex - er - - ci -

- tus An - - ge - lo - - - - rum: qui - a sa - lus__ ae - ter - - na_____

hu - ma - - - no ge - ne - ri_____ ap - - - - - - - - - - - - -

Verse (Soloists)

- pa - ru - - - - it.__ Glo - ri - a_____ in ex - cel - sis__ De - - -

- o,__ et in ter - ra pax ho - mi - ni - bus bo - nae_____ vo - lun - ta - - - tis.__

The responsory is repeated from *Gaudet* to the end.

Gloria Patri (Soloists)

Glo - ri - a_____ Pa - tri,__ et___ Fi - li - - - o,__ et Spi - ri - - tu -

- i__ San - - - - - cto.__

The entire responsory is sung again.

LU, pp. 375–6.

A *responsory* or *respond* was sung after each of the three or nine lessons at Matins. It normally consisted of the choral responsory itself, a solo psalm verse, and a choral repetition of the second half of the responsory, but on major feasts a solo performance of the *Gloria Patri* and a final choral statement of the entire responsory were added to the scheme. Responsorial chants tended to be florid, allowing time for meditation on the preceding lesson.

TRANSLATION
Today the King of heaven has deigned to be born of a Virgin for us, so that He may recall lost mankind to the heavenly kingdom; the angelic army rejoices, for eternal safety has appeared to humankind. Glory be to God on high, and in earth peace towards men of good will. Glory be to the Father, and to the Son, and to the Holy Ghost.

9. *Tract* Qui confidunt in Domino

Tract at Mass on the fourth Sunday of Lent (Gregorian)

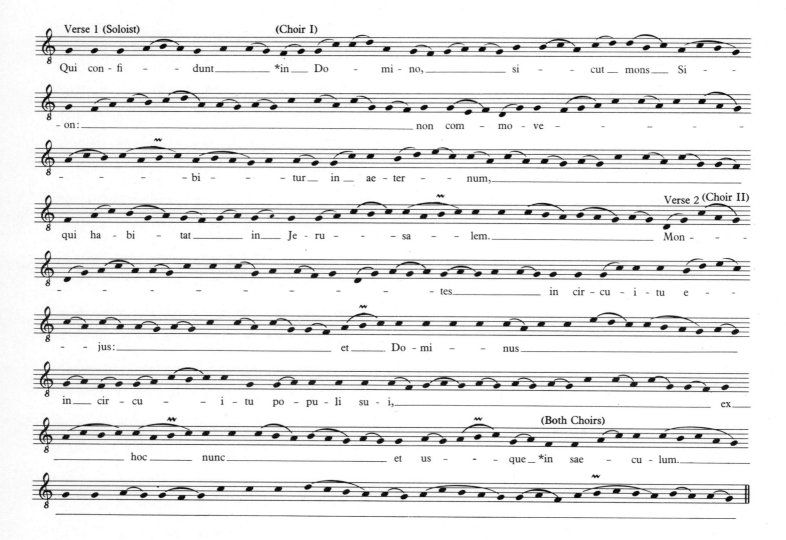

LU, pp. 561–2.

The *tract* was one of the few examples of *direct psalmody* – i.e. psalmody without extraneous material – which survived into the medieval period. It replaced the alleluia in the mass for the dead and on certain other occasions. Originally a solo chant, it came to consist of a florid setting of several psalm verses performed *alternatim* by the choir. There were relatively few tract melodies, a high proportion of which show evidence of *centonization* – i.e. of being made up from a basic repository of melodic formulae.

TRANSLATION
They that put their trust in the Lord shall be even as the Mount Sion: which may not be removed, but standeth fast for ever, which stands by Jerusalem. The hills stand about Jerusalem, and the Lord about His people, from this time forth for evermore.

10. *Procession before Mass of the Day on Easter Day*

According to the customs of Salisbury Cathedral

The procession was formed at the quire-step [see page 27 for diagram]. It was headed by two or more virgers who were followed by a boy carrying holy water, three acolytes carrying crosses, two candle-bearers, two censer-bearers, a sub-deacon and deacon carrying the Epistles and Gospels, the priest, the choirboys, and the clerics with the most senior members at the rear. At the quire-step three clerks of the highest form sang in the middle of the choir the *refrain of the processional hymn* Salve, festa dies *which the choir, led by the precentor, repeated. The three clerks then sang the first verse and the procession moved off. Leaving the quire by the west door, it went down the middle of the nave and out of the church by the main west door. Turning north, it proceeded round the outside of the church and cloisters, reentering the church [probably] through the Canons' Door, passing the font and moving back up the nave. During this procession the three clerks sang the verses of the hymn and the choir sang the refrain after every verse.*

10a. *Processional hymn* Salve, festa dies

The ending of the hymn was intended to coincide with the arrival of the procession before the rood. Here a halt or station was made. The antiphon Sedit angelus *was begun by the precentor and taken up by the choir. Three clerks of the highest form sang the verse* Crucifixum in carne *from the rood loft, turning towards the congregation in the nave. The antiphon was then repeated from 'Nolite'.*

10b. *Processional antiphon* Sedit angelus

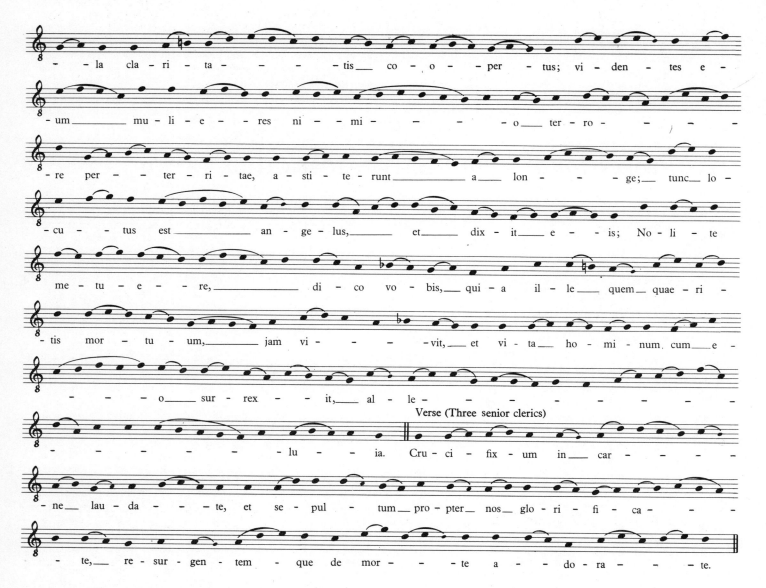

-la cla-ri-ta - - - - - tis___ co - o - per - tus; vi - den - tes e -
-um___ mu-li-e-res ni - - mi - - - - - o___ ter-ro - - - - -
-re per - - ter-ri-tae, a - sti - te - runt_____ a - lon - - - ge;___ tunc__ lo -
-cu - tus est_____ an - ge - lus,_____ et___ dix - it e - - is; No - li - te
me - tu - e - - re,_____ di - co vo - bis,___ qui - a il - le___ quem__ quae - ri -
-tis mor - tu - um,_____ jam vi - - - - vit,___ et vi - ta__ ho - mi - num. cum e -
- - - - o___ sur - rex - - it,___ al - le - - - - - - - - -
- - - - - - - - lu - - ia.   Cru - ci - fix - um in___ car - - - - - - -

Verse (Three senior clerics)

-ne lau - da - - - te, et se - pul - tum__ pro - pter__ nos__ glo - ri - fi - ca - - -
-te,___ re - sur - gen - tem - que de mor - - - te a - - do - ra - - - te.

As the procession re-entered the quire the precentor began the antiphon Christus
resurgens *which, with its verse and alleluia, was sung by the whole choir.*

10c. *Processional antiphon* Christus resurgens

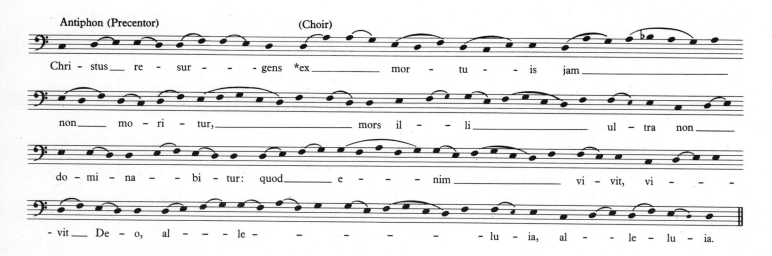

Antiphon (Precentor)   (Choir)

Chri - stus___ re - sur - - - gens *ex_____ mor - tu - - is jam_____
non_____ mo - ri - tur,_____ mors il - - li_____ ul - tra non____
do - mi - na - - bi - tur: quod_____ e - - nim_____ vi - vit, vi - - -
-vit___ De - o, al - - le - - - - - - - - lu - ia, al - - le - lu - ia.

Verse

Di - cant nunc Ju - dae - i, quo - mo - do mi - li - tes cu - sto - di - en - tes se - pul - chrum per - di - de - runt re - gem ad la - pi - dis po - si - ti - o - nem, qua - re non ser - va - bant pe - tram ju - sti - ti - ae; aut se - pul - tum red - dant, aut re - sur - gen - tem a - do - rent, no - bis - cum di - cen - tes, al - le - lu - ia, al - le - lu - ia.

When the procession had returned to the quire-step it ended with this versicle, response, and prayer.

10d. *Versicle*

Versicle (Most important person present)

Sur - rex - it Do - mi - nus de se - pul - chro, al - le - lu - ia, al - le - lu - ia.

Response (Choir)

Qui pro no - bis per - pen - dit in lig - no, al - le - lu - ia, al - le - lu - ia.

10e. *Prayer*

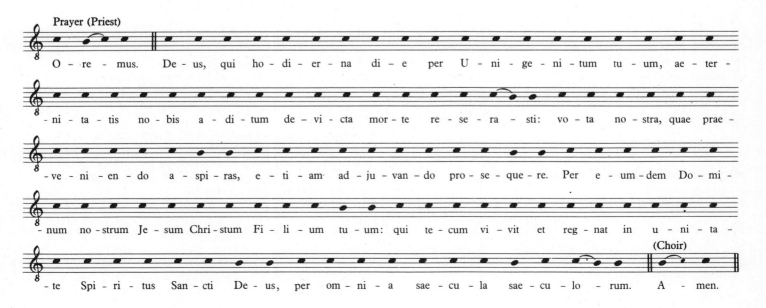

Prayer (Priest)

O - re - mus. De - us, qui ho - di - er - na di - e per U - ni - ge - ni - tum tu - um, ae - ter - ni - ta - tis no - bis a - di - tum de - vi - cta mor - te re - se - ra - sti: vo - ta no - stra, quae prae - ve - ni - en - do a - spi - ras, e - ti - am ad - ju - van - do pro - se - que - re. Per e - um - dem Do - mi - num no - strum Je - sum Chri - stum Fi - li - um tu - um: qui te - cum vi - vit et reg - nat in u - ni - ta - te Spi - ri - tus San - cti De - us, per om - ni - a sae - cu - la sae - cu - lo - rum. (Choir) A - men.

The celebration of Mass followed at once.

The description is paraphrased from the rubrics in W. G. Henderson, *Processionale ad usum . . . Sarum* (Leeds, 1882), pp. 92–94, and in US, I.

The importance of processions in medieval church worship is not always appreciated. Processions took place usually before Matins or Mass or after Vespers on major feast days. They normally began at the quire-step and moved around the inside or outside of the church or even from one church to another. The main constituents were a processional hymn, several antiphons or responsories, and a final prayer. The processions of Salisbury cathedral were especially elaborate. Like many medieval cathedrals, Salisbury built up a set of liturgical customs and material which, although essentially Roman, was sufficiently distinctive to be recognized as an independent rite. The resulting Salisbury liturgy was adopted in many English churches after about 1200 and even found its way on to the continent. York, Hereford, and Lincoln were among other English dioceses to have their own uses or liturgies.

10a: London, British Library, MS Harley 2942, ff. 54v–56r.

A processional hymn with refrain. It had several sets of verses, for use on different occasions. In a hymn each verse was usually sung to the same melody.
TRANSLATION
Hail thee, Festival Day! blest day that art hallowed for ever; Day wherein God o'ercame hell and arose from the dead.
   Lo, the fair beauty of earth, from the death of the winter arising, Every good gift of the year now with its Master returns.
He who was nailed to the Cross is God and the Ruler of all things; All things created on earth worship the Maker of all.
God of all pity and power, let Thy word be assured to the doubting; Light on the third day returns: rise, Son of God, from the tomb!
Ill doth it seem that Thy limbs should linger in lowly dishonour, Ransom and price of the world, veiled from the vision of men.
Ill it beseemeth that Thou, by whose hand all things are encompassed, Captive and bound should remain, deep in the gloom of the rock.
Rise now, O Lord, from the grave and cast off the shroud that enwrapped Thee; Thou art sufficient for us: nothing without Thee exists.
Mourning they laid Thee to rest, who art Author of life and creation; Treading the pathway of death, life Thou bestowedst on man.
Show us Thy face once more, that the ages may joy in Thy brightness; Give us the light of day, darkened on earth at Thy death.
Out of the prison of death Thou art rescuing numberless captives; Freely they tread in the way whither their Maker has gone.
Jesus has harrowed hell; he has led captivity captive: Darkness and chaos and death flee from the face of the light.

10b: AS, pl. 242.

An antiphon from the procession at Matins on Easter Day.
TRANSLATION
The angel sat at the tomb of the Lord, clad in a shining garment. Seeing him, the women were seized with great terror and stood a long way off. Then the angel spoke and said to them: 'Fear not, I say to you, for He that you seek dead now lives, and the life of men is risen with Him, alleluia.' Praise Him, crucified on the Cross, and glorify Him, buried for us; adore Him, risen from the dead.

10c: AS, pl. 241.

An antiphon also taken from the procession at Matins on Easter Day.
TRANSLATION
Christ being raised from the dead, dieth no more; death hath no more dominion over Him; for in that He liveth, He liveth unto God. Alleluia, Alleluia. Now let the Jews declare, how the soldiers who kept the sepulchre lost the King when the stone was rolled, wherefore kept they not the rock of righteousness; let them either produce the buried, or adore the risen One, saying with us, Alleluia, Alleluia.

10d: AS, pl. 249.

A *versicle and response* taken from the procession at Matins on Easter Day.
TRANSLATION
The Lord is risen from the grave, alleluia, alleluia. Who for us hung on the Tree, alleluia, alleluia.

10e: US, II, p. lxxvj.
The collect for Mass on Easter Day (translated in note 11d).

Glossary

Acolyte: A junior member of a church, often intended for the priesthood, who assisted during services by carrying vessels etc.
Burse: Receptacle in which the corporal cloths and offertory-veil were kept.
Cantoris: Those of the choir sitting on the north side of the quire with the precentor.
Chalice: Goblet containing the water and wine during the Eucharist.
Clerk of the first form: One of the most junior clerics or lay-clerks. The choir-boys sat on the same form.
Clerk of the highest form: A senior cleric, either an important dignitary of the church or a canon high in the order of precedence.
Clerk of the second form: A junior cleric, inferior to the dignitaries and senior canons of the highest form; also a lay-clerk – i.e. a singer not in holy orders deputizing in services for a member of the church.
Cope: A long cloak worn by ecclesiastics in processions and on occasions of special solemnity.
Corporal cloth: A cloth on which the consecrated elements were placed during Mass.
Decani: Those of the choir sitting on the south side of the quire with the dean.
Offertory-veil: A cloth used to cover the chalice.
Paten: A plate or dish on which the bread was placed during Mass.
Pax-board: A board or ornament handed round as a substitute for the kiss of peace. Each member of the choir kissed it and then handed it on to his neighbour.
Precentor: The chief musical official of a church, responsible for the conduct of the plainsong items in the services.
Pulpitum: A lectern situated on the rood-loft, above the doorway between quire and nave. Sometimes there were also lecterns at the quire-step and in the centre of the quire.
Pyx: A container in which the consecrated bread was kept.
Quire: The part of the church where the choir assisted during services.
Ruler: A member of the choir chosen to assist the precentor or to act in his place.
Versicle and Response: A short dialogue, usually between celebrant and choir, sung to a simple plainsong formula.

Simplified plan of Salisbury Cathedral

1 High altar, with altar-steps in front, at sides, and behind
2 Sedilia (seats) for celebrants
3 Relics
4 Presbytery-step
5 North door of quire and presbytery
6 South door of quire and presbytery
7 Quire-step
8 Clerks of the highest form
9 Clerks of the second form
10 Clerks of the first form and choirboys
11 Doorway between quire and nave, with cross and pulpitum (rood loft) above
12 Vestibulum (sacristy)
13 Chapter house
14 Cloisters
15 Font
16 West door
17 Cross in church-yard
18 Canons' door

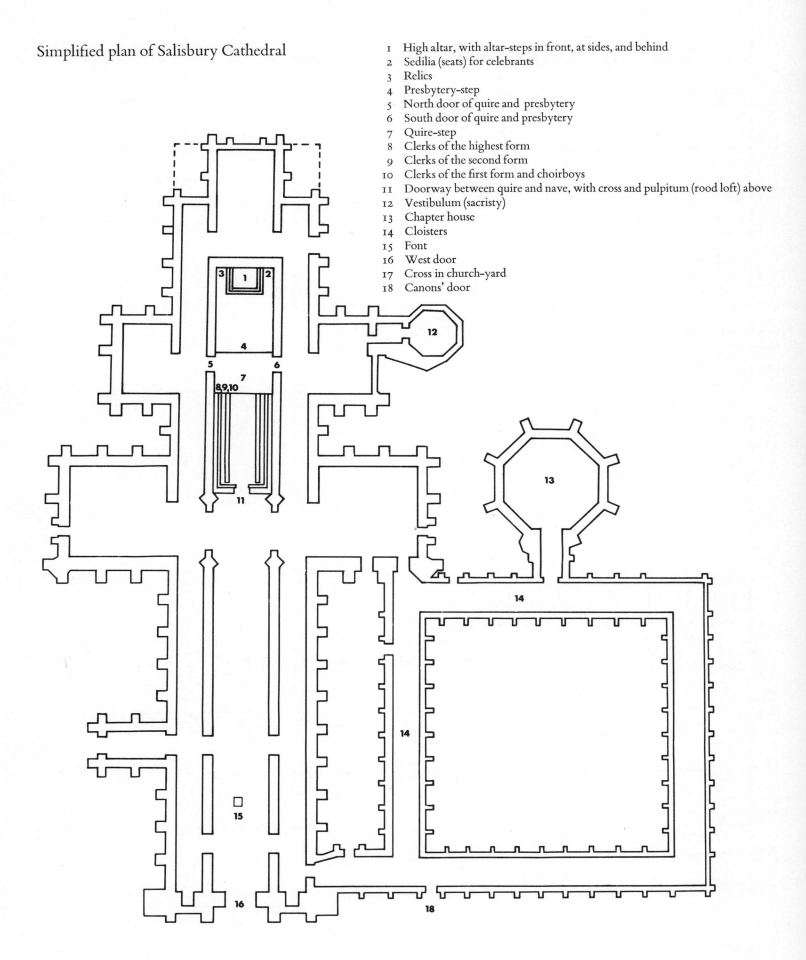

11. *Mass of the Day on Easter Day*

According to the customs of Salisbury Cathedral

Immediately before Mass the priest and his assistants robed in the vestry. As they did so the priest said the hymn Veni, Creator Spiritus *[see No. 95] and the following items.*

VERSICLE (PRIEST):
Emitte Spiritum tuum et creabuntur.

RESPONSE (ASSISTANTS):
Et renovabis faciem terrae.

PRAYER (PRIEST):
Deus, cui omne cor patet et omnis voluntas loquitur, et quem nullum latet secretum, purifica per infusionem Sancti Spiritus cogitationes cordis nostri, ut te perfecte diligere et digne laudare mereamur. Per Dominum nostrum Jesum Christum, Filium tuum, qui tecum vivit et regnat in unitate ejusdem Spiritus Sancti, Deus: per omnia saecula saeculorum.

(ASSISTANTS):
Amen.

ANTIPHON (PRIEST):
Introibo ad altare Dei.

PSALM 42 (PRIEST AND ASSISTANTS ALTERNATELY):
Judica me Deus, et discerne causam meam de gente non sancta: ab homine iniquo et doloso erue me.
Quia tu es Deus fortitudo mea: quare me repulisti, et quare tristis incedo, dum affligit me inimicus?
Emitte lucem tuam, et veritatem tuam: ipsa me deduxerunt, et adduxerunt in montem sanctum tuum et in tabernacula tua.

Et introibo ad altare Dei: ad Deum qui laetificat juventutem meam.
Confitebor tibi in cithara, Deus, Deus meus: quare tristis es anima mea, et quare conturbas me?
Spera in Deo, quoniam adhuc confitebor illi: salutare vultus mei, et Deus meus.
Gloria Patri, et Filio, et Spiritui Sancto.
Sicut erat in principio, et nunc, et semper: et in saecula saeculorum. Amen.

ANTIPHON (PRIEST):
Introibo ad altare Dei.
RESPONSE (ASSISTANTS):
Ad Deum qui laetificat juventutem meam.

(PRIEST):
Kyrie eleison. Christe eleison. Kyrie eleison.

(PRIEST):
Pater noster, qui es in caelis: Sanctificetur nomen tuum: Adveniat regnum tuum: Fiat voluntas tua, sicut in caelo, et in terra. Panem nostrum quotidianum da nobis hodie: Et dimitte nobis debita nostra, sicut et nos dimittimus debitoribus nostris.

At this point the celebration of Mass actually began as the choir, already in their places in the quire, commenced the Introit. The Introit and following Kyrie accompanied the progress of the priest and his ministers from the vestry to the altar and the words and actions which followed. The choir had to stand, except during the Epistle, Gradual, and Sequence, when they were allowed to sit. From the Sanctus to 'Pax Domini sit semper vobiscum' the choir knelt.

11a. Introit (Officium)

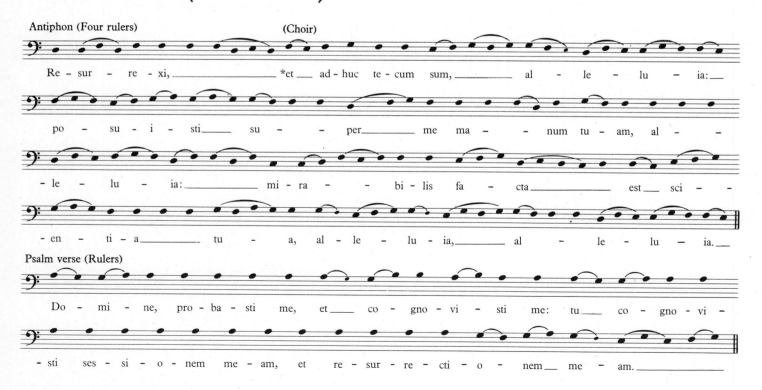

The choir repeated the antiphon.

Gloria Patri (Rulers)

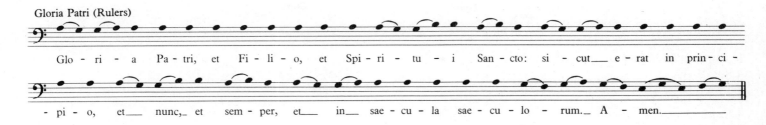

Glo - ri - a Pa - tri, et Fi - li - o, et Spi - ri - tu - i San - cto: si - cut _ e - rat in prin - ci -

- pi - o, et _ nunc, _ et sem - per, et _ in _ sae - cu - la sae - cu - lo - rum. _ A - men. _

The choir repeated the antiphon again.
The Kyrie, with the trope Deus creator, followed at once.

11b. Kyrie *with trope* Deus Creator

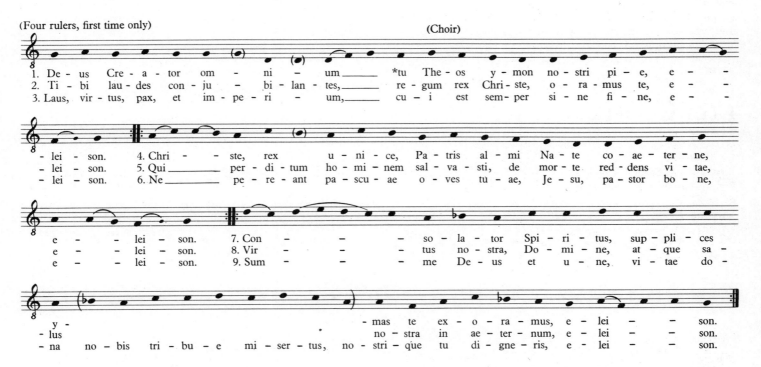

(Four rulers, first time only)   (Choir)

1. De - us Cre - a - tor om — ni — um _____ *tu The - os y - mon no - stri pi - e, e —
2. Ti - bi lau - des con - ju — bi - lan - tes, _____ re - gum rex Chri - ste, o - ra - mus te, e —
3. Laus, vir - tus, pax, et im - pe - ri — um, _____ cu - i est sem - per si - ne fi - ne, e —

- lei - son. 4. Chri — ste, rex u - ni - ce, Pa - tris al - mi Na - te co - ae - ter - ne,
- lei - son. 5. Qui ____ per - di - tum ho - mi - nem sal - va - sti, de mor - te red - dens vi - tae,
- lei - son. 6. Ne ____ pe - re - ant pa - scu - ae o - ves tu - ae, Je - su, pa - stor bo - ne,

e — - lei - son. 7. Con — — — so - la - tor Spi - ri - tus, sup - pli - ces
e — - lei - son. 8. Vir — — — tus no - stra, Do - mi - ne, at - que sa -
e — - lei - son. 9. Sum — — me De - us et u - ne, vi - tae do -

y -   - mas te ex - o - ra - mus, e - lei — — son.
- lus   no - stra in ae - ter - num, e - lei — — son.
- na no - bis tri - bu - e mi - ser - tus, no - stri - que tu di - gne - ris, e - lei — — son.

Meanwhile, as soon as the Gloria Patri of the Introit had been begun, the priest and his assistants entered the presbytery and approached the altar in the following order: firstly two candle-bearers, then a censer-bearer, five subdeacons [the principal one carrying the Epistles], five deacons [the principal one carrying the Gospels] and lastly the priest. At the altar-step the priest said confession, the principal deacon and subdeacon assisting on his right and left.

(PRIEST):

Et ne nos inducas in tentationem.

(DEACON AND SUBDEACON):

Sed libera nos a malo.

(P):

Confitemini Domino quoniam bonus.

(D AND S):

Quoniam in saeculum misericordia ejus.

(P):

Confiteor Deo, beatae Mariae, omnibus Sanctis, et vobis; quia peccavi nimis cogitatione, locutione, et opere: mea culpa: precor sanctam

Mariam, omnes Sanctos Dei, et vos, orare pro me.

(D AND S):

Misereatur vestri omnipotens Deus, et dimittat vobis omnia peccata vestra; liberet vos ab omni malo; conservet et confirmet in bono; et ad vitam perducat aeternam.

(P):

Amen.

(D AND S):

Confiteor (as above).

(P):

Misereatur (as above).

(D AND S):

Amen.

(P):

Absolutionem et remissionem omnium peccatorum vestrorum, spatium verae paenitentiae, et emendationem vitae, gratiam et consolationem Sancti Spiritus, tribuat vobis omnipotens et misericors Dominus.

(D AND S):
Amen.
(P):
Adjutorium nostrum in nomine Domini.
(D AND S):
Qui fecit caelum et terram.
(P):
Sit nomen Domini benedictum.
(D AND S):
Ex hoc nunc et usque in saeculum.
(P):
Oremus.

After praying, the priest kissed the deacon and subdeacon, saying
Habete osculum pacis et dilectionis, ut apti sitis sacrosancto altari, ad perficiendum officia divina.

The acolytes set down their candles at the altar-step and the priest moved up to stand in front of the middle of the altar. Bowing and joining his hands, he said in a low voice
Oremus. Aufer a nobis, quaesumus, Domine, cunctas iniquitates nostras, ut ad Sancta sanctorum puris mereamur mentibus introire. Per Christum Dominum nostrum. Amen.

Then he stood upright, kissed the altar and signed the cross before his face, saying
In nomine Patris et Filii et Spiritus Sancti. Amen.

After the Introit one of the candle-bearers brought bread, water and wine for the eucharist and the other brought a basin with water and a towel. The principal deacon prepared to place incense in the censer, saying to the priest
(DEACON):
Benedicite.

(PRIEST):
Dominus. Ab ipso bene✝dicatur in cujus honore cremabitur. In nomine Patris et Filii et Spiritus Sancti. Amen.
The deacon placed incense in the censer and gave it to the priest who censed the altar and was himself censed by the deacon. The priest then kissed the Epistles held by the subdeacon, after which he, the deacon and subdeacon retired to their seats south of the altar until the choir had finished the Kyrie. After the Kyrie the priest returned to the centre of the altar and began the Gloria. This was continued by the choir as the priest moved back to the south side and said the text privately with his ministers. At 'Gloria in excelsis', 'adoramus', 'suscipe', and 'Jesu Christe' the choir turned and bowed to the altar. At 'in gloria Dei Patris' the choir crossed themselves.

11c. Gloria

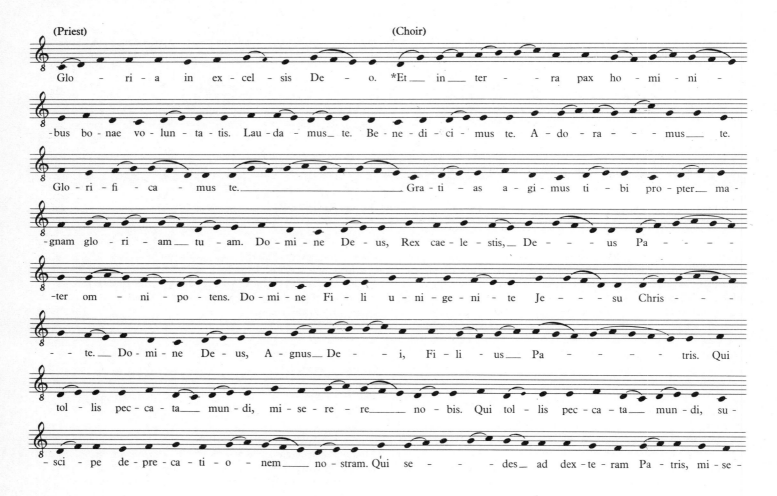

-re — re___ no - bis. Quo - ni - am__ tu so - lus sanc-tus. Tu so - lus Do - mi - nus. Tu so -
-lus al - tis - si - mus, Je — — su Chri — — — - ste.__ Cum San - - - cto Spi — — —
-ri - tu, in glo - ri - a De - i Pa — — tris. A — — — — — — — men.__

After the Gloria the priest crossed himself. Turning towards the people with his arms raised a little and with his hands joined, he sang

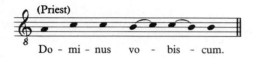

(Priest)

Do - mi - nus vo - bis - cum.

(Choir)

Et cum Spi - ri - tu tu - o.

Turning to the altar, the priest sang the Collect of the day.

11d. Collect (Oratio)

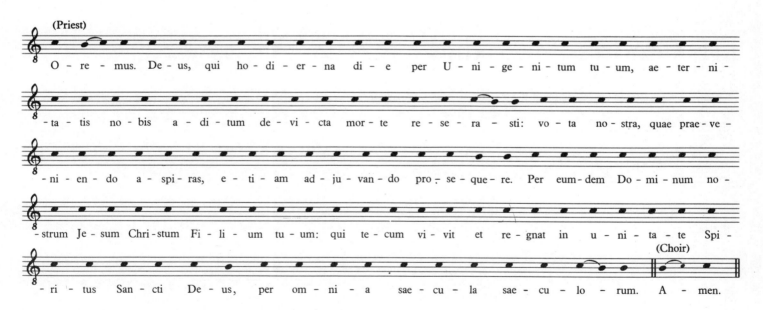

(Priest)

O - re - mus. De - us, qui ho - di - er - na di - e per U - ni - ge - ni - tum tu - um, ae - ter - ni -

-ta - tis no - bis a - di - tum de - vi - cta mor - te re - se - ra - sti: vo - ta no - stra, quae prae - ve -

-ni - en - do a - spi - ras, e - ti - am ad - ju - van - do pro - se - que - re. Per eum - dem Do - mi - num no -

-strum Je - sum Chri - stum Fi - li - um tu - um: qui te - cum vi - vit et re - gnat in u - ni - ta - te Spi -

(Choir)

-ri - tus San - cti De - us, per om - ni - a sae - cu - la sae - cu - lo - rum. A - men.

If any more Collects or Memorials were to be said, the priest repeated 'Oremus' and sang the remaining prayers one after another with 'Per omnia . . .' after only the last of them. Clergy were allowed to enter the quire to participate in Mass up to the end of the first Collect. As the final Collect was begun the principal subdeacon came through the middle of the quire to read the Epistle from the lectern on the rood-loft or pulpitum.

11e. Epistle

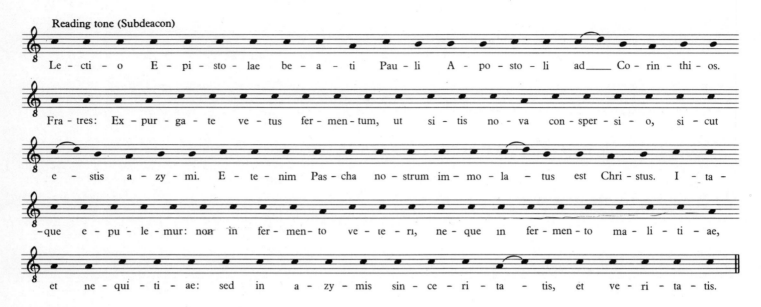

Reading tone (Subdeacon)

Le - cti - o E - pi - sto - lae be - a - ti Pau - li A - po - sto - li ad___ Co - rin - thi - os.

Fra - tres: Ex - pur - ga - te ve - tus fer - men - tum, ut si - tis no - va con - sper - si - o, si - cut

e - stis a - zy - mi. E - te - nim Pas - cha no - strum im - mo - la - tus est Chri - stus. I - ta -

-que e - pu - le - mur: non in fer - men- to ve - te - ri, ne - que in fer - men - to ma - li - ti - ae,

et ne - qui - ti - ae: sed in a - zy - mis sin - ce - ri - ta - tis, et ve - ri - ta - tis.

During the Epistle two of the acolytes took up their candles and escorted the third acolyte as he brought the chalice, paten, offertory-veil, and corporal cloths from the presbytery to the altar. As he retired he kissed the altar and the bearers replaced the candles. Meanwhile three clerks of the second form bowed to the altar from the quire-step and went up into the rood-loft, ready to begin the Gradual when the Epistle ended. After the Epistle one of the candle-bearers and a choirboy prepared the lectern in the rood-loft for the Gospel reading.

11f. Gradual Haec dies

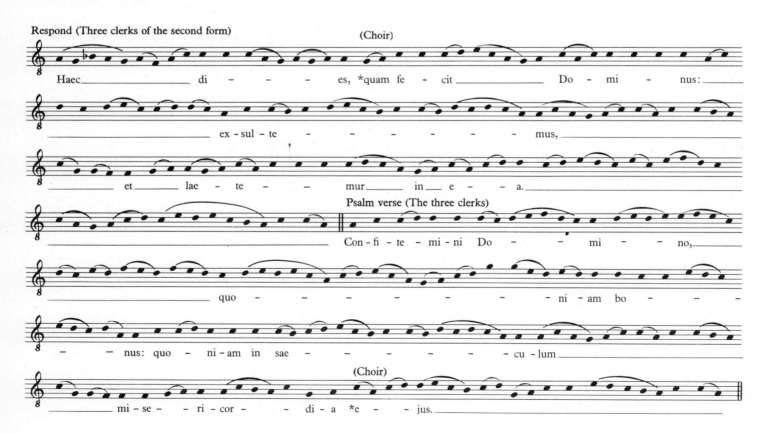

Respond (Three clerks of the second form)   **(Choir)**

Haec___ di - - - es, *quam fe - cit ___ Do - mi - - nus:___

ex - sul - te - - - - - mus,

et___ lae - te - mur___ in e - a.___

Psalm verse (The three clerks)

Con - fi - te - mi - ni Do - - mi - no,___

quo - - - - - - - ni - am bo - - -

- nus: quo - ni - am in sae - - - - cu - lum___

(Choir)

mi - se - ri - cor - di - a *e - - jus.___

The choir was allowed to sit during the Epistle and Gradual. While it was being sung three clerks of the highest form donned silken copes in the vestry and went through the middle of the quire up into the rood-loft, ready to begin the Alleluia. After the Gradual the three second-formers bowed to the altar and returned to their places, and the three seniors began the Alleluia.

11g. *Alleluia* Pascha nostrum

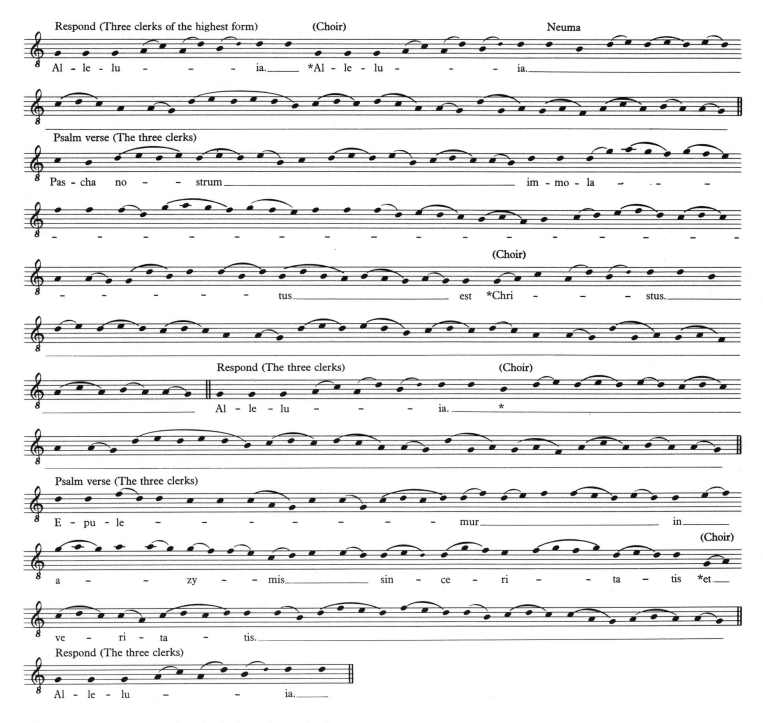

After the Alleluia the three seniors bowed to the altar and returned to the vestry to remove their copes, afterwards resuming their places in the choir. The Sequence followed, being begun by the rulers and continued by the choir alternatim, with both sides of the choir singing the last verse.

11h. *Sequence* Fulgens praeclara

(Rulers)　　　　　　　　　　　　(Choir, decani alternating with cantoris; all sang last verse)

1. Ful - gens_____ *prae - - - - cla - ra ru - ti - lat per or - bem ho -
2. De ho - ste su - per - bo quem

-di - e di - es, in qua Chri - sti lu - ci - da nar - ran - tur o - van - ter__ prae - li - a.
Je - sus tri - um - pha - vit, pul - chre ca - stra il - li - us pe - ri - mens te - ter - ri - ma.

3. In - fe - lix cul - pa E - vae, qua ca - ru - i - mus om - nes vi - ta.　5. Be - ne - di - cta sit cel -
4. Fe - lix pro - les Ma - ri - ae, qua e - pu - la - mur mo - do u - na.　6. Ge - ne - rans Re - gem spo -

-sa Re - gi - na il - la,　7. Pol - len - tem jam in ae - the - ra. Rex in ae - ter - num__ su -
-li - an - tem tar - ta - ra,　8. Pa - tris se - dens ad dex - te - ram, Vi - ctor u - bi - que__ mor -

-sci - pe be - ni - gnus prae - co - ni - a no - stra se - du - le ti - bi ca - nen - ti - a,
-te su - pe - ra - ta, at - que tri - um - pha - ta, po - lo - rum pos - si - dens__ gau - di - a.

9. O ma - gna, O cel - sa, O pul - chra, cle - men - ti - a Chri - sti lu - ci - flu -
10. Laus ti - bi ho - nor - que ac vir - tus, qui__ no - stram an - ti - quam le - vi - a -

-a,__ O al - ma.　11. Ro - se - o cru - o - re A - gni be - ni - gnis - si - mi em - pta flo -
-sti__ sar - ci - nam.　12. Po - ten - ti vir - tu - te no - stra qui la - vit fa - ci - no - ra tri -

-ri - da mi - cat__ haec au - la.　13. Stu - pens val - de in me - met jam mi - ror ho -
-bu - ens do - na__ ful - gi - da.　14. Tan - ta__ in - di - gnis pan - de - re no - bis sa -

-di - er - na.　15. Stir - pe Da - vi - ti - ca or - tus, de tri - bu Ju - da Le - o__ po -
-cra - men - ta.　16. Fun - dens o - lim ar - va, re - gna pe - tis su - pe - ra, ju - stis__ red -

-tens__ sur - rex - i - sti in__ glo - ri - a, A - gnus vi - sus es in ter - ra.
-dens__ prae - mi - a, in__ sae - cu - la di - gnan - ter o - van - ti - a.

17. Dic, im - pi - e Za - bu - le, quid va - let nunc__ fraus tu - a,　19. Tri - bus,__ lin - guae, ad - mi -
18. I - gne - is nex - us ·lo - ris a Chri - sti vi - cto - ri - a?　20. Ut mors__ mor - tem sic su -

(1) F, E second time　(2) E, D second time

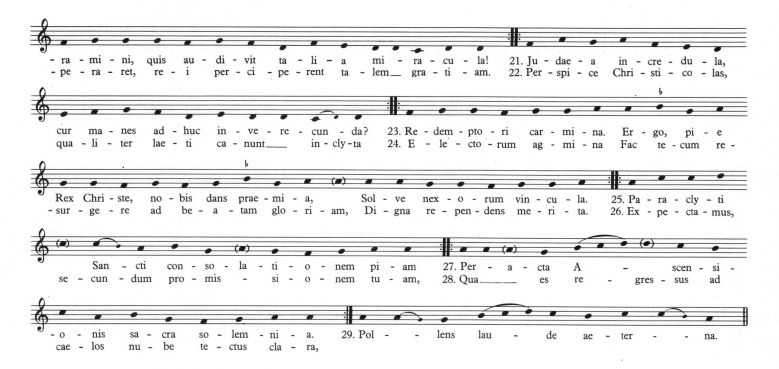

-ra - mi - ni, quis au - di - vit ta - li - a mi - ra - cu - la! 21. Ju - dae - a in - cre - du - la,
-pe - ra - ret, re - i per - ci - pe - rent ta - lem gra - ti - am. 22. Per - spi - ce Chri - sti - co - las,

cur ma - nes ad - huc in - ve - re - cun - da? 23. Re - dem - pto - ri car - mi - na. Er - go, pi - e
qua - li - ter lae - ti ca - nunt in - cly - ta 24. E - le - cto - rum ag - mi - na Fac te - cum re -

Rex Chri - ste, no - bis dans prae - mi - a, Sol - ve nex - o - rum vin - cu - la. 25. Pa - ra - cly - ti
-sur - ge - re ad be - a - tam glo - ri - am, Di - gna re - pen - dens me - ri - ta. 26. Ex - pe - cta - mus,

San - cti con - so - la - ti - o - nem pi - am 27. Per - a - cta A - scen - si
se - cun - dum pro - mis - si - o - nem tu - am, 28. Qua es re - gres - sus ad

-o - nis sa - cra so - lem - ni - a. 29. Pol - lens lau - de ae - ter - na.
cae - los nu - be te - ctus cla - ra,

Meanwhile, when the priest and his assistants had said the Gradual, Alleluia, and Sequence to themselves, the principal deacon washed his hands, placed the corporals on the altar, placed the bread on the paten and poured water and wine into the chalice, asking the seated priest to bless the water.

(DEACON):
Benedicite.

(PRIEST):
Dominus. Ab eo sit bene✠dicta, de cujus latere exivit sanguis et aqua. In nomine Patris et Filii et Spiritus Sancti. Amen.

The deacon censed the altar and presented the Gospels to the priest who was now standing before the altar.

(DEACON):
Jube Domine benedicere.

(PRIEST):
Dominus sit in corde et in ore tuo ad pronunciandum sanctum Evangelium Dei. In nomine Patris et Filii et Spiritus Sancti. Amen.

Preceded by the candle-bearers, censer-bearer, and cross-bearer, the deacon went through the middle of the quire bearing the Gospels solemnly in his left hand. On reaching the rood-loft the principal subdeacon took the text and held it on the deacon's left for him to read. The cross-bearer stood on the deacon's right, the candle-bearers on either side, and the censer-bearer behind him. The deacon signed the cross with his thumb over the book, his face, and breast, saying

(Deacon)
Do - mi - nus vo - bis - cum.

(Choir)
Et cum spi - ri - tu tu - o.

He then read the Gospel, facing northwards. The choir turned towards the altar and then towards him.

11j. Gospel (Evangelium)

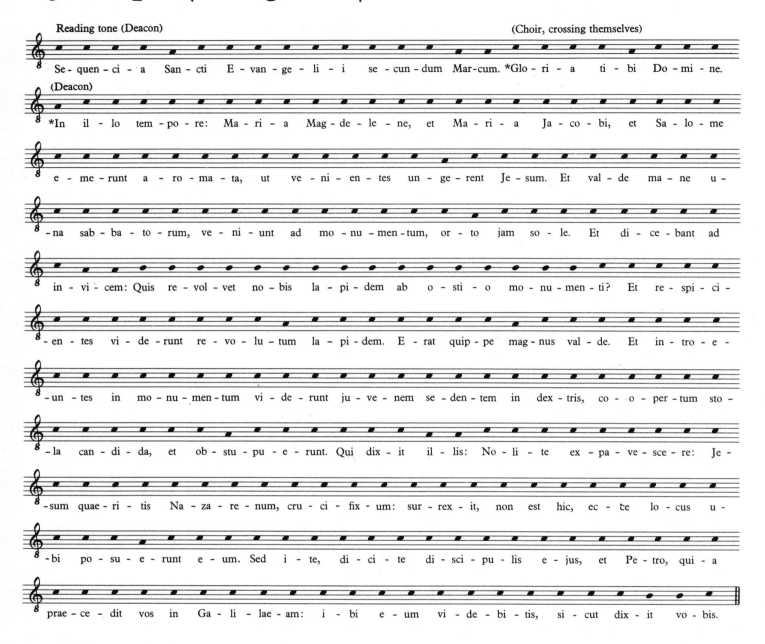

After reading the Gospel the deacon kissed the book, took it from the subdeacon
(who kissed his right hand) and carried it against his breast back to the altar.
Meanwhile the priest stood before the altar and began the Credo. When the
deacon came to the priest he offered him the Gospels to kiss. At the beginning of
the Credo the choir crossed themselves and bowed to the altar, bowing also at
'et incarnatus', 'et homo', 'crucifixus', and 'vitam venturi'. The choir
continued to face the altar, except during the Offertory, for the rest of the Mass.

11k. Credo

(Priest)

Do - mi - nus vo - bis - cum.

(Choir)

Et cum spi - ri - tu tu - o.

(Priest)

O - re - mus.

The rulers began the Offertory.

111. *Offertory* Terra tremuit

Antiphon (Rulers) (Choir)

Ter - ra *tre - mu - it, et qui - e - vit, dum re -

- sur - ge - ret in ju - di - ci - o De - us, al -

- le - lu - ia

The deacon gave the priest the chalice with the paten and host (or wafer or sacrifice), kissing his hand each time. The priest took the chalice with the paten and host placed upon it and put it on the middle of the altar. He bowed and raised the chalice a little, offering the host to the Lord and saying

Suscipe, Sancta Trinitas, hanc oblationem, quam ego indignus peccator offero in honore tuo, beatae Mariae et omnium Sanctorum tuorum, pro peccatis et offensionibus meis: et pro salute vivorum et requie omnium fidelium defunctorum. In nomine Patris et Filii et Spiritus Sancti acceptum sit omnipotenti Deo hoc sacrificium novum.

He replaced the chalice and covered it with the corporal cloth. Then he slid the host off the paten on to the corporal cloth in front of the chalice, afterwards kissing the paten and placing it under the corporal cloth to the right of the chalice. He took the censer from the deacon and censed the host, signing the cross thrice above it, thrice around the chalice and on both sides of the host and chalice, then thrice between the altar and himself. As he censed he said
Dirigatur, Domine, ad te oratio mea, sicut incensum in conspectu tuo.

The priest was censed by the deacon and the subdeacon brought him the Gospels to kiss. An acolyte censed the choir, beginning with the precentor and rulers and proceeding in descending order of seniority, bowing to each cleric as he censed him. A subdeacon followed with the Gospels for everybody to kiss. After the censing the priest went to the south side of the altar and washed his hands, saying
Munda me, Domine, ab omni inquinamento mentis et corporis; ut possim mundus implere opus sanctum Domini.

Meanwhile the deacon censed the north side of the altar and the relics. The priest returned to stand before the altar and the deacon and subdeacon returned to their respective steps. Bowing and joining his hands, the priest said
In spiritu humilitatis et in animo contrito suscipiamur, Domine, a te: et sic fiat sacrificium nostrum in conspectu tuo, ut a te suscipiatur hodie, et placeat tibi, Domine Deus meus.

Rising, he kissed the altar to the right of the host. Blessing the host, he crossed himself and said
In nomine Patris et Filii et Spiritus Sancti. Amen.

He turned to the people and said in a low voice
Orate, fratres et sorores pro me, ut meum pariterque vestrum acceptum sit Domino Deo nostro sacrificium.

The clerics answered to themselves
Sancti Spiritus gratia illuminet cor tuum et labia tua, et accipiat Dominus digne hoc sacrificium laudis de manibus tuis pro peccatis et offensionibus nostris.

Turning to the altar, the priest said the Secret.
Oremus. Suscipe, quaesumus Domine, preces populi tui cum oblationibus hostiarum: ut paschalibus initiatae mysteriis, ad aeternitatis nobis medelam, te operante, proficiant. Per Dominum nostrum Jesum Christum Filium tuum, qui tecum vivit et regnat, in unitate Spiritus Sancti, Deus.

(Priest)

Per om - ni - a sae - cu - la sae - cu - lo - rum.

(Choir)

A - men.

(Priest)

Do - mi - nus vo - bis - cum.

(Choir)

Et cum spi - ri - tu__ tu - o.

When the priest began 'per omnia' the subdeacon took the paten and offertory-veil from the deacon. Covering the former with the latter he handed both to an acolyte to hold until the Pater noster, *the acolyte standing on the step behind him. The priest lifted his hands and sang*

(Priest)

Sur - sum cor - da.__

(Choir)

Ha - be - mus ad__ Do - mi - num.__

(Priest)

Gra - ti - as a - ga - mus Do - mi - no__ De - o no - stro.

(Choir)

Di - gnum et__ ju - stum est.__

11m. Proper preface for Easter Day

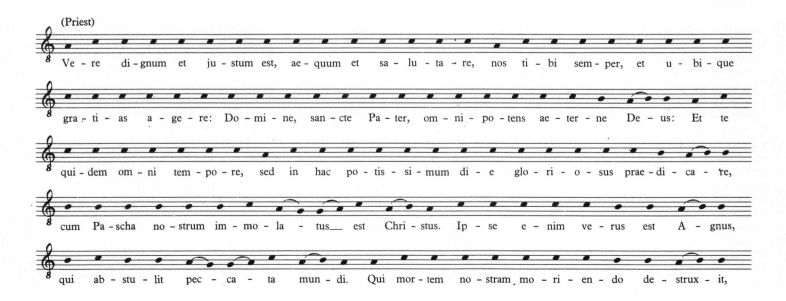

(Priest)

Ve - re di - gnum et ju - stum est, ae - quum et sa - lu - ta - re, nos ti - bi sem - per, et u - bi - que

gra - ti - as a - ge - re: Do - mi - ne, san - cte Pa - ter, om - ni - po - tens ae - ter - ne De - us: Et te

qui - dem om - ni tem - po - re, sed in hac po - tis - si - mum di - e glo - ri - o - sus prae - di - ca - re,

cum Pa - scha no - strum im - mo - la - tus__ est Chri - stus. Ip - se e - nim ve - rus est A - gnus,

qui ab - stu - lit pec - ca - ta mun - di. Qui mor - tem no - stram mo - ri - en - do de - strux - it,

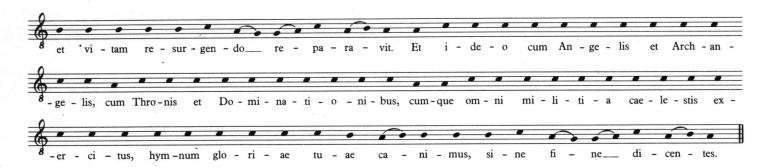

et ʼvi - tam re - sur - gen - do re - pa - ra - vit. Et i - de - o cum An - ge - lis et Arch - an -

-ge - lis, cum Thro - nis et Do - mi - na - ti - o - ni - bus, cum - que om - ni mi - li - ti - a cae - le - stis ex -

-er - ci - tus, hym - num glo - ri - ae tu - ae ca - ni - mus, si - ne fi - ne di - cen - tes.

The rulers immediately began the Sanctus and a bell was rung thrice. The priest raised his joined hands until 'in nomine Domini' when he crossed himself. The choir crossed themselves at 'Benedictus'.

11n. Sanctus

(Rulers)   (Choir)

San - - - - - - ctus, *San - - - - - ctus, San - - - -

- - - - ctus Do - mi - nus De - us Sa - ba - oth. Ple - ni sunt cae - li et ter -

-ra glo - ri - a tu - a. Ho - san - na in ex - cel - sis. Be - ne - di - ctus qui

ve - nit in no - mi - ne Do - mi - ni. Ho - san - na in ex - cel - sis.

After the Sanctus the priest joined his hands and raised his eyes, saying Te igitur, clementissime Pater, per Jesum Christum Filium tuum Dominum nostrum, supplices rogamus [*bowing*] ac petimus, [*rising and kissing the altar to the right of the host*] uti accepta habeas, et benedicas [*signing three crosses over the chalice and host*] haec do✠na, haec mu✠nera, haec san✠cta sacrificia illibata [*raising his hands*] in primis, quae tibi offerimus pro Ecclesia tua sancta catholica: quam pacificare, custodire, adunare, et regere digneris toto orbe terrarum: una cum famulo tuo Papa nostro N. et Antistite nostro N. et Rege nostro N. et omnibus orthodoxis, atque catholicae et apostolicae fidei cultoribus.

Memento, Domine, famulorum famularumque tuarum N. et N.; [*here praying five times – for himself, his relations, his friends and parishioners, all those present, and all Christian people*] et omnium circumstantium, quorum tibi fides cognita est et nota devotio, pro quibus tibi offerimus: vel qui tibi offerunt hoc sacrificium laudis, pro se, suisque omnibus: pro redemptione animarum suarum, pro spe salutis, et incolumitatis suae: tibique reddunt vota sua aeterno Deo, vivo et vero. Communicantes, et diem sacratissimum celebrantes Resurrectionis Domini nostri Jesu Christi secundum carnem: sed et memoriam venerantes, in primis gloriosae semper Virginis Mariae, Genetricis ejusdem Dei et Domini nostri Jesu Christi: sed et beatorum Apostolorum ac Martyrum tuorum, Petri, Pauli, Andreae, Jacobi, Johannis, Thomae, Jacobi, Philippi, Bartholomaei, Mattaei, Simonis et Thaddaei: Lini, Cleti, Clementis, Xysti, Cornelii, Cypriani, Laurentii, Chrysogoni, Johannis et

Pauli, Cosmae et Damiani: et omnium Sanctorum tuorum; quorum meritis, precibusque concedas, ut in omnibus protectionis tuae muniamur auxilio. Per eumdem Christum Dominum nostrum. Amen.

[*Regarding the host with great reverence*] Hanc igitur oblationem servitutis nostrae, sed et cunctae familiae tuae quam tibi offerimus, pro his quoque quos regenerare dignatus es ex aqua et Spiritu Sancto, tribuens eis remissionem omnium peccatorum, quaesumus, Domine, ut placatus accipias: diesque nostros in tua pace disponas, atque ab aeterna damnatione nos eripi, et in electorum tuorum jubeas grege numerari. Per Christum Dominum nostrum. Amen.

[*Again regarding the host*] Quam oblationem tu Deus omnipotens in omnibus, quaesumus, [*signing three crosses over the host and chalice*] bene✠dictam, adscri✠ptam, ra✠tam, rationabilem, acceptabilemque facere digneris: ut nobis [*signing the cross over the host*] Cor✠pus, [*and over the chalice*] et San✠guis [*joining his hands*] fiat dilectissimi Filii tui Domini nostri Jesu Christi. [*Raising his joined hands, then wiping his fingers and elevating the host*] Qui pridie quam pateretur, accepit panem in sanctas ac venerabiles manus suas, et elevatis oculis in caelum, [*raising his eyes*] ad te Deum Patrem suum omnipotentem, [*bowing, then rising a little*] tibi gratias agens, bene✠dixit, fregit, [*touching the host*] deditque discipulis suis, dicens: Accipite, et manducate ex hoc omnes. Hoc est enim corpus meum.

The last sentence was said in a single breath. The priest then bowed to the host, elevated it above his forehead to be seen by the people, signed the cross with it, and replaced it before the chalice. Then he uncovered the chalice and held it between his hands, keeping thumb and forefinger joined except to sign the cross, saying

Simili modo postquam cenatum est, accipiens et hunc praeclarum Calicem in sanctas ac venerabiles manus suas: item tibi [*bowing*] gratias agens, bene✠dixit deditque discipulis suis, dicens: Accipite et bibite ex eo omnes. [*Lifting the chalice a little*] Hic est enim Calix sanguinis mei, novi et aeterni testamenti: mysterium fidei: qui pro vobis et pro multis effundetur in remissionem peccatorum. [*Raising it to his breast or above his head*] Haec quotiescumque feceritis, in mei memoriam facietis.

He replaced the chalice and rubbed his fingers over it to remove any crumbs. He covered it and raised his arms to form a cross, joining his fingers and saying
Unde et memores, Domine, nos tui servi, sed et plebs tua sancta, ejusdem Christi Filii tui Domini Dei nostri tam beatae passionis, nec non et ab inferis resurrectionis, sed et in caelos gloriosae ascensionis: offerimus praeclarae majestati tuae de tuis donis ac datis, [*signing five crosses – three over the host and chalice, one over the host, and one over the chalice*] hostiam pu✠ram, hostiam san✠ctam, hostiam immacu✠latam, Pa✠nem sanctum vitae aeternae, et Cali✠cem salutis perpetuae.
Supra quae propitio ac sereno vultu respicere digneris: et accepta habere, sicuti accepta habere dignatus es munera pueri tui justi Abel, et sacrificium Patriarchae nostri Abrahae: et quod tibi obtulit summus sacerdos tuus Melchisedech, sanctum sacrificium, immaculatam hostiam. [*Bowing and crossing his hands*] Supplices te rogamus, omnipotens Deus: jube haec perferri per manus sancti Angeli tui in sublime altare tuum, in conspectu divinae majestatis tuae: ut quotquot, [*rising and kissing the altar to the right of the host*] ex hac altaris participatione sacrosanctum Filii

tui [*signing the cross over the host*] Cor✠pus, [*and over the chalice*] et San✠guinem sumpserimus, omni [*and before his face*] bene✠dictionem caelesti et gratia repleamur. Per eumdem Christum Dominum nostrum. Amen.

Memento etiam, Domine, animarum famulorum, famularumque tuarum N. et N., qui nos praecesserunt cum signo fidei, et dormiunt in somno pacis. Ipsis, Domine, et omnibus in Christo quiescientibus, locum refrigerii, lucis et pacis, ut indulgeas, deprecamur. Per eumdem Christum Dominum nostrum. Amen.

[*Striking his breast*] Nobis quoque peccatoribus famulis tuis, de multitudine miserationum tuarum sperantibus, partem aliquam, et societatem donare digneris, cum tuis sanctis Apostolis et Martyribus: cum Johanne, Stephano, Matthia, Barnaba, Ignatio, Alexandro, Marcellino, Petro, Felicitate, Perpetua, Agatha, Lucia, Agnete, Caecilia, Anastasia, et omnibus Sanctis tuis: intra quorum nos consortium, non aestimator meriti, sed veniae, quaesumus, largitor admitte. Per Christum Dominum nostrum. Per quem haec omnia, Domine, semper bona creas, [*signing the cross thrice above the chalice*] sancti✠ficas, vivi✠ficas, bene✠dicis, et praestas nobis.

He uncovered the chalice and signed the cross five times with the host – firstly beyond the chalice on both sides, then in a line with it, then below it, then as at first, lastly before it. Meanwhile the deacon, having washed his hands, stood on the priest's right to help him lift the corporal; when he retired he kissed the altar and the priest's right shoulder as the latter said
Per ip✠sum, et cum ip✠so, et in ip✠so, est tibi Deo Patri omni✠potenti, in unitate Spiritus✠Sancti omnis honor et gloria.
Then he covered the chalice and, keeping his hands above the altar until he began the Pater noster, *he sang*

(Priest)
Per om-ni-a sae-cu-la sae-cu-lo-rum.

(Choir)
A-men.

(Priest)
O-re-mus. Prae-ce-ptis sa-lu-ta-ri-bus mo-ni-ti, et di-vi-na in-sti-tu-ti-o-ne for-ma-ti, au-de-mus di-ce-re:

The deacon meanwhile took the paten from the subdeacon and held it uncovered and on high with his arms extended, standing on the priest's right. The priest raised his hands and sang

11p. Pater noster

(Priest)
Pa-ter no-ster, qui es in cae-lis: San-cti-fi-ce-tur＿ no-men tu-um: Ad-ve-ni-at

re - gnum tu - um: Fi - at vo - lun - tas tu - a, si - cut in cae - lo,__ et__ in ter - ra. Pa - nem no -
-strum quo - ti - di - a - num da no - bis ho - di - e: et di - mit - te no - bis de - bi - ta no - stra, si - cut et
nos di - mit - ti - mus de - bi - to - ri - bus no - stris. Et ne nos in - du - cas in ten - ta - ti - o - nem.

(Choir)
Sed li - be - ra nos a ma - lo.

The priest said 'Amen' to himself and then prayed
Libera nos, quaesumus Domine, ab omnibus malis, praeteritis,
praesentibus, et futuris: et intercedente beata et gloriosa semper Virgine
Dei Genetrice Maria, et beatis Apostolis tuis Petro et Paulo atque Andrea,
cum omnibus Sanctis,

*Here the deacon gave the paten to the priest, kissing his hand. The priest kissed
the paten, held it before his left eye and his right eye, signed the cross with it
above his head and replaced it before the altar. He continued*
Da propitius pace in diebus nostris: ut ope misericordiae tuae adjuti, et a
peccato simus semper liberi, et ab omni perturbatione securi.

*The priest uncovered the chalice and, bowing, took the host between his thumbs
and forefingers and broke it into three parts as he said*
[*At the first fraction*] Per eumdem Dominum nostrum Jesum Christum
Filium tuum. [*At the second fraction*] Qui tecum vivit et regnat in unitate
Spiritus Sancti Deus.

*He held two portions of the host in his left hand, and the third in his right hand
above the chalice, singing*

(Priest)
Per om - ni - a sae - cu - la sae - cu - lo - rum.

(Choir)
A - men.

*The priest signed the cross three times within the chalice with the third portion of
the host, singing*

(Priest)
Pax Do - mi - ni ✠ sit sem ✠ per vo ✠ bis - cum.

(Choir)
Et cum spi - ri - tu tu - o.

*The Agnus Dei followed, the deacon and subdeacon coming to the priest's right
hand to say the text privately with him. The priest put the two portions of the
host in his left hand onto the paten.*

11q. Agnus Dei

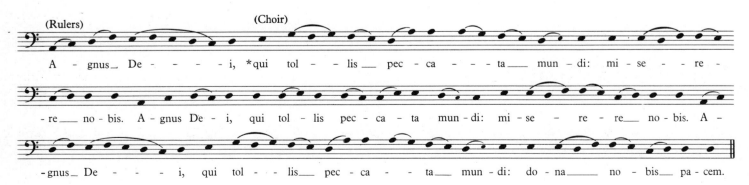

(Rulers) (Choir)
A - gnus__ De - - - i, *qui tol - - lis__ pec - ca - - ta__ mun - di: mi - se - - re -
- re__ no - bis. A - gnus De - i, qui tol - - lis pec - ca - ta mun - di: mi - se - re - re__ no - bis. A -
-gnus__ De - - - i, qui tol - - lis__ pec - ca - - ta__ mun - di: do - na____ no - bis__ pa - cem.

Signing the cross, the priest put the third portion of the host into the chalice, saying
Haec sacro✠sancta commixtio Corporis et Sanguinis Domini nostri Jesu Christi fiat mihi omnibusque sumentibus salus mentis et corporis, et ad vitam aeternam promerendam et capescendam praeparatio salutaris. Per eumdem Christum Dominum nostrum. Amen.

Domine, sancte Pater, omnipotens aeterne Deus, da mihi hoc sacrosanctum Corpus et Sanguinem Filii tui Domini nostri Jesu Christi ita digne sumere ut merear per hoc remissionem omnium peccatorum meorum accipere et tuo Sancto Spiritu repleri; et pacem tuam habere; quia tu es Deus solus et praeter te non est alius, cujus regnum et imperium gloriosum sine fine permanet in saecula saeculorum. Amen.

The priest kissed the corporal cloths on the right of and above the chalice and then gave the deacon the kiss of peace, saying
(PRIEST):
Pax tibi et Ecclesiae Dei.

(DEACON):
Et cum spiritu tuo.

The deacon gave the kiss of peace to the subdeacon and then carried the pax-board to the rulers of the choir. It was then passed round the choir. Meanwhile the priest prayed privately, holding the host in both hands.
Deus Pater, fons et origo totius bonitatis, qui ductus misericordia Unigenitum tuum pro nobis ad infima mundi descendere et carnem sumere voluisti, quam ego indignus hic in manibus meis teneo, [*bowing to the host*] te adoro, te glorifico, te tota mentis ac cordis intentione laudo et precor; ut nos famulos tuos non deseras, sed peccata nostra dimittas, quatenus tibi soli vivo ac vero Deo, puro corde et casto corpore, servire valeamus. Per eumdem Christum Dominum nostrum. Amen.

Domine Jesu Christe, Fili Dei vivi, qui ex voluntate Patris, cooperante Spiritu Sancto, per mortem tuam mundum vivificasti: libera me, quaeso, per hoc sacrosanctum Corpus et hunc Sanguinem tuum a cunctis iniquitatibus meis et ab universis malis: et fac me tuis semper obedire mandatis, et a te nunquam in perpetuum separari permittas, Salvator mundi: qui cum Deo Patre et eodem Spiritu Sancto vivis et regnas Deus per omnia saecula saeculorum. Amen.

Corporis et Sanguinis tui, Domine Jesu Christe, sacramentum, quod licet indignus accipio, non sit mihi judicio et condemnationi: sed tua prosit pietate corporis mei et animae saluti. Amen.

Before receiving the host he addressed it, bowing and saying
Ave in aeternum, sanctissima caro Christi, mihi ante omnia et super omnia summa dulcedo. Corpus Domini nostri Jesu Christi sit mihi peccatori via et vita. In no✠mine Patris et Filii et Spiritus Sancti. Amen.
He signed the cross with the host before his mouth and then received it, afterwards bowing and addressing the blood thus:
Ave in aeternum, caelestius potus, mihi ante omnia et super omnia summa dulcedo. Corpus et Sanguis Domini nostri Jesu Christi prosint mihi peccatori ad remedium sempiternum in vitam aeternam. Amen. In no✠mine Patris et Filii et Spiritus Sancti. Amen.

He received the blood.
Then he went to the south side of the altar with the chalice between his hands, his fingers joined as before. The subdeacon poured wine and then water into the chalice and the priest washed any crumbs from his fingers, saying
Quod ore sumpsimus, Domine, pura mente capiamus: et de munere temporali fiat nobis remedium sempiternum.

He washed his fingers in the wine in the chalice and drank the wine, saying
Haec nos communio, Domine, purget a crimine, et caelestis remedii faciat esse consortes.

The subdeacon poured water into the chalice. The priest drank it and, returning to stand before the altar, bowed and said
Gratias tibi ago, Domine, sancte Pater, omnipotens aeterne Deus, qui me refecisti de sacratissimo Corpore et Sanguine Filii tui Domini nostri Jesu Christi: et precor, ut hoc sacramentum salutis nostrae quod sumpsi indignus peccator, non veniat mihi ad judicium neque ad condemnationem pro meritis meis: sed ad profectum corporis mei et animae saluti in vitam aeternam. Amen.

The priest went to the south side of the altar and washed his hands while the deacon folded the corporals. The subdeacon took up the Epistles. If any liquid remained in the chalice the deacon then gave it to the priest to drink. After this the Communion was sung, the priest and his ministers saying it privately.

11r. *Communion* Pascha nostrum

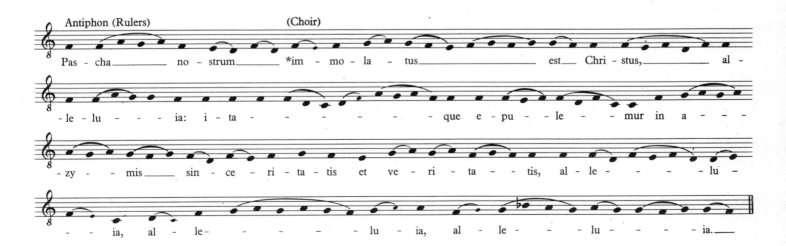

Antiphon (Rulers)   (Choir)
Pas - cha no - strum *im - mo - la - tus est Chri - stus, al -
-le - lu - ia: i - ta - que e - pu - le - mur in a - -
-zy - mis sin - ce - ri - ta - tis et ve - ri - ta - tis, al - le - lu -
- ia, al - le - lu - ia, al - le - lu - ia.

After the Communion the priest turned to the people, signed the cross before his
face and sang, with his arms raised a little and his hand joined,

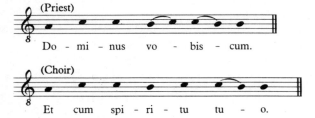

Turning to the altar, he sang the Postcommunion.

11S. Postcommunion

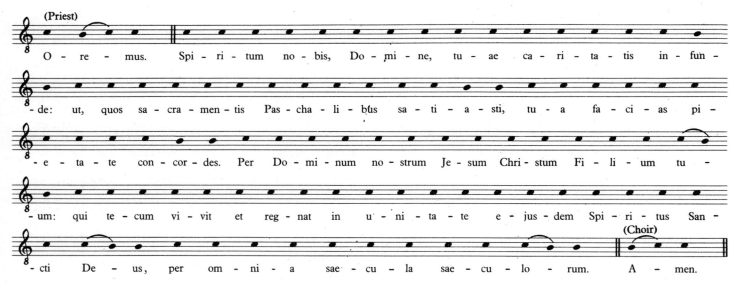

When the priest sang 'Per omnia' the deacon gave the chalice, paten,
offertory-veil, and corporals to an acolyte, who bore them away with the same
ceremony as that with which he had brought them. The priest signed the cross
before his face and turned to the people, singing

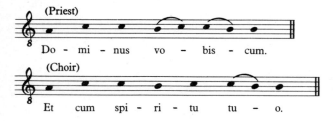

The deacon turned to the people and sang

11t. Ite missa est

(Deacon)

I - - - te,_____ mis - - sa___ est.

(Choir)

De - - - o_____ gra - - ti - as.

Bowing and joining his hands, the priest prayed in a low voice.
Placeat tibi, sancta Trinitas, obsequium servitutis meae: et praesta; ut hoc sacrificium, quod oculis tuae majestatis indignus obtuli, tibi sit acceptabile, mihique, et omnibus, pro quibus illud obtuli, sit, te miserante, propitiabile. Qui vivis et regnas Deus per omnia saecula saeculorum. Amen.

He rose, signed the cross before his face and said
In nomine Patris et Filii et Spiritus Sancti. Amen.
Then he and his ministers bowed to the altar and departed in the order in which they had come, as the priest recited from the Gospel of St John, chapter I, verses 1–14, after which the ministers said 'Deo gratias'.

The description is paraphrased from the rubrics in US, I, pp. 61–90, and in F. H. Dickinson, *Missale ad usum . . . Sarum* (Burntisland, 1861–83). Translations are taken from *The Sarum Missal in English* (London, 1868).

Whereas the Daily Office was celebrated only once a day, Mass could be conducted any number of times. Mass of the Day was the main celebration, attended by the entire religious community of the church. The musical constituents of Mass were of two kinds – the Ordinary, whose texts never changed although their music was variable, and the Proper, whose texts and music altered according to the festival being celebrated. Sung texts formed only a small part of the texts of the Mass and were, in fact, largely a commentary on and adornment of the essential words and actions. Mass at Salisbury cathedral differed slightly from Roman Mass in some of its text and ritual, tending towards greater elaboration. The reader will notice the detail and precision of the rubric over matters whose importance is not immediately apparent. Despite the fact that much of the celebrant's activity took place during the musical items, a medieval Mass was a lengthy affair. The degree of ceremony and elaboration with which it was carried through depended upon the solemnity of the feast day. Mass on Easter Day was one of the most elaborate and magnificent celebrations, both in the extent of its ritual and in the expansive style of many of its sung items. Reference to the diagram on page 27 will enable readers to visualize the course of the ceremony.

11a: GS, pl. K.

The Introit, Offertory, and Communion were the *antiphonal* chants of Mass. Originally each had been a complete psalm with antiphon but most of the psalm verses had disappeared at an early date. Thus the Introit retained a single psalm verse and the *Gloria Patri*, while by the 13th century the Offertory and Communion were reduced to the antiphon alone (although the Communion of the Mass for the dead still had a psalm verse).
TRANSLATION
When I wake up, I am present with Thee, Alleluia. Thou hast laid Thy hand upon me, Alleluia. Such knowledge is too wonderful for me, Alleluia. O Lord, Thou hast searched me out, and known me: Thou knowest my down-sitting, and mine up-rising. Glory be to the Father, and to the Son, and to the Holy Ghost: as it was in the beginning, is now, and ever shall be, world without end. Amen.

11b: GS, pl. 1+ and 2+.

The Western church adopted the Kyrie from the Eastern church probably during the 6th century and retained the Greek language of the text, which consisted of a threefold invocation 'Kyrie-Christe-Kyrie eleison', each invocation being stated thrice. During and after the 9th century the Kyrie was frequently sung in a *troped* form – i.e. supplied with additional text, music, or both to make it especially appropriate to a particular occasion. *Deus Creator* was the grandest of the English Kyrie tropes and was reserved for feasts of the greatest solemnity.
TRANSLATION
O Divine Creator of all things, Thou our God, in Thy pity, have mercy upon us.
Unto Thee, O Christ, the King of kings, rejoicing in praise together, we pray Thee, have mercy upon us.
Thou to whom ever belongeth praise, virtue, peace, and dominion without end, have mercy upon us.
O Christ, King, only Son, coeternal with Thy gracious Father, have mercy upon us.
Thou who didst save lost man, restoring him from death unto life, have mercy upon us.
Jesu, the Good Shepherd, that the sheep of Thy pasture perish not, have mercy upon us.
O Spirit, the Comforter, we Thy suppliants most humbly beseech Thee, have mercy upon us.
O Lord our strength and our salvation evermore, have mercy upon us.
O Supreme and one God, bestow on us the gifts of life in Thy compassion, and deign to have mercy upon us.

11c: GS, pl. 11+ and 12+.

The Gloria also was taken over from the Byzantine liturgy. The length of the text caused most of its melodies to be syllabic and simple in style, often consisting of two or three motives repeated with slight variation. The Gloria was not sung in Advent or from Septuagesima to Easter.
TRANSLATION
Glory be to God on high. And in earth peace towards men of good will. We praise Thee. We bless Thee. We worship Thee. We glorify Thee. We give thanks to Thee for Thy great glory. O Lord God, heavenly King, God the Father Almighty. O Lord, the only-begotten Son Jesu Christ. O Lord God, Lamb of God. Thou that takest away the sins of the

world, have mercy upon us. Thou that takest away the sins of the world, receive our prayer. Thou that sittest at the right hand of the Father, have mercy upon us. For Thou only art holy. Thou only art the Lord. Thou only, O Jesu Christ, art most high. With the Holy Ghost, in the glory of God the Father. Amen.

11d: US, II, p. lxxvj.

Collects or prayers were intoned on a monotone inflected at the ends of sentences.
TRANSLATION
God, who on this day through Thine Only-begotten hast overcome death, and opened unto us the gate of everlasting life; as by preventing us Thou dost put into our minds good desires, so by Thy help bring the same to good effect. Through Jesus Christ our Lord, who with Thee and the Holy Ghost liveth and reigneth, ever one God, world without end. Amen.

11e: US, I, 265–266.

The Epistle and Gospel had their own reading tones which were rather more elaborate than the tone for the Collect.
TRANSLATION
The reading from the Epistle of the blessed apostle Paul to the Corinthians. Purge out therefore the old leaven, that ye may be a new lump, as ye are unleavened. For even Christ our passover is sacrificed for us: therefore let us keep the feast, not with old leaven, neither with the leaven of malice and wickedness; but with the unleavened bread of sincerity and truth.

11f: GS, pl. 117.

The Gradual and Alleluia were the *responsorial* chants of mass. At first they had consisted of a solo performance of a psalm punctuated by a choral refrain or *responsory*. As in the antiphonal chants, however, most of the psalm verses had disappeared from the scheme by the late Middle Ages. Thus the Gradual had a choral responsory and a solo verse, the responsory being repeated on some occasions. Responsorial chants were often of an elaborate if not virtuosic nature, allowing time for meditation.
TRANSLATION
This is the day which the Lord hath made: we will rejoice and be glad in it. O give thanks unto the Lord for He is gracious, because His mercy endureth for ever.

11g: GS, pl. 117.

See note 11f. The Alleluia for Easter Day was one of the few to retain a second solo verse. By the 14th century, however, this had been discarded. Both verses were paraphrased from the Epistle for the day.
TRANSLATION
Alleluia. Christ our passover is sacrificed. Let us keep the feast with the unleavened bread of sincerity and truth.

11h: London, British Library, MS Lansdowne 462, ff. 50v–51v.

Sequences arose out of the medieval practice of *troping* – i.e. of adding words, music, or both to an existing plainchant. During the 9th century the Sequence, which had begun as a trope of the *neuma* (final melisma) of the Alleluia, became an independent form. It consisted of a number of paired verses, each pair being sung to a repeated musical phrase. The musical form aa, bb, cc etc. resulted. Sometimes there was an unpaired verse at the beginning and/or at the end. Troping and Sequence composition continued throughout the later Middle Ages, and were eventually proscribed by the Council of Trent (1545–63).
TRANSLATION
This day the dawn glows bright above the sun, Telling how Christ hath fought and glorious victory won. Jesus hath triumphed o'er the haughty foe, And his foul camp majestic hath laid low. Unhappy sin of Eve, Of which all death do reap; O happy Mary's Child With whom now feast we keep. Blest be the Queen exalted high, His Mother, Who triumphantly Hath spoiled hell and reigneth in the sky. O King for ever, graciously Accept the praise we offer Thee, To Thee at God's Right Hand on high, Crying aloud incessantly. Thou, death's power now overthrown, Triumphing on high art gone, To joys of Heaven which are Thine own. O vast, O fair, O high, Light-giving clemency, Breathing benignantly! Honour to Thee and praise who didst that load upraise Which burdened our old days. Brightly shine the courts of God Purchased by the crimson flood Of the Lamb's most precious Blood. By His mighty virtue He Cleansed all our misery, Granting gifts benign and free. Awestruck within myself I gaze Upon the wonders of these days, That before our unworthy eyes Such mighty sacraments should rise. From the root of David springing, Of Judah's tribe the Lion Thou Hast arisen, glory bringing, Who didst seem a Lamb but now. Thou who laid'st the earth's foundations Seekest now the realms on high, To eternal generations Recompensing righteously. Prince of evil, wicked fiend, What avails thy impious lie? In fiery chains thou art confined By Christ's glorious victory. Ye peoples, marvel at the tale! Whoe'er such miracles hath heard? That death o'er death should so prevail, Such grace on sinners be conferred! Judea, unbelieving land, Look forth and on the Christians gaze, See how in joyous crowds they stand And chant the blest Redeemer's praise! Wherefore, O Christ, our holy King, Loose us from guilt, and pardon bring. Grant that Thy chosen bands with Thee May rise in blest felicity, And of Thy grace rewarded be. The Holy Paraclete's blest comfort, Lord, We look for, trusting to Thy gracious word, Soon as Ascension's holy day In solemn joy hath passed away, When Thou, returning to the skies, Oe'rshadowed by a cloud to endless praise didst rise.

11j: US, I, pp. 266–267.

see note 11e.
TRANSLATION
The holy Gospel according to St Mark. Thanks be to Thee, O Lord. At that time Mary Magdalene, and Mary the mother of James, and Salome, had bought sweet spices, that they might come and anoint Him. And very early in the morning the first day of the week, they came unto the sepulchre at the rising of the sun. And they said among themselves, Who shall roll us away the stone from the door of the sepulchre? And when they looked, they saw that the stone was rolled away: for it was very great. And entering into the sepulchre, they saw a young man sitting on the right side, clothed in a long white garment; and they were affrighted. And he saith to them, Be not affrighted: Ye seek Jesus of Nazareth, which was crucified: He is risen; He is not here: behold the place where they laid Him. But go your way, tell His disciples and Peter that He goeth before you into Galilee: there shall ye see Him, as He said unto you.

11k: GS, pl. C & D.

Another item from the Byzantine liturgy, the Credo was established in the Roman mass only in the early 11th century although it had appeared in the Gallican and Mozarabic masses several hundred years earlier. There was only one Salisbury Credo melody, although the Roman liturgy contained several, some of which were clearly related. As in the Gloria, the length of the text prompted a simple and repetitive melodic type.

TRANSLATION
I believe in one God, the Father Almighty, Maker of heaven and earth, and of all things visible and invisible. And in one Lord Jesus Christ, the only-begotten Son of God. Begotten of His Father before all worlds. God of God, Light of Light, Very God of Very God. Begotten, not made, being of one substance with the Father: by Whom all things were made. Who for us men, and for our salvation came down from heaven.

And was incarnate by the Holy Ghost of the Virgin Mary: and was made man. And was crucified for us under Pontius Pilate: He suffered, and was buried. And the third day He rose again according to the Scriptures. And ascended into heaven: and sitteth on the right hand of the Father. And He shall come again with glory to judge both the quick and the dead: whose kingdom shall have no end. And I believe in the Holy Ghost, The Lord and Giver of Life: who proceedeth from the Father and the Son. Who with the Father and the Son together is worshipped and glorified: who spake by the Prophets. And I believe one Holy Catholic and Apostolic Church. I acknowledge one Baptism for the remission of sins. And I look for the Resurrection of the dead. And the life of the world to come. Amen.

11l: GS, pl. 117.

See note 11a.
TRANSLATION
The earth trembled and was still, when God arose to judgement. Alleluia.

11m: F. H. Dickinson, *Missale ad Usum Insignis et Praeclarae Ecclesiae Sarum* (Burntisland, 1861–83), pp. 599–600 and 608–10.

The Proper Preface preceded the Sanctus. It was sung to a reading tone and changed its text slightly according to the occasion.
TRANSLATION
It is very meet, right, just, and our bounden duty, that we should at all times and in all places give thanks unto Thee, O Lord Holy Father Almighty, everlasting God: and Thee indeed at all seasons, but chiefly on this day, ought we more gloriously to praise, since Christ our passover is sacrificed for us. For He is the very Lamb which hath taken away the sins of the world, Who by His death hath destroyed Death, and by His rising to life again hath restored to us Life. Therefore with Angels and Archangels, with Thrones and Dominions, and with all the company of the Heavenly Host we magnify Thy glorious Name, evermore saying

11n: GS, pl. 15+.

The Sanctus entered the Western liturgy from Byzantium probably during the 6th century. On major feast days it was sung to a moderately elaborate melody, but on less important occasions simpler melodies were used.
TRANSLATION
Holy, Holy, Holy Lord God of Hosts. Heaven and earth are full of Thy glory. Hosanna in the highest. Blessed is he that cometh in the Name of the Lord. Hosanna in the highest.

11p: US, pp. 270–271.
TRANSLATION
Our Father, which art in heaven, Hallowed be Thy Name: Thy kingdom come: Thy will be done on earth as it is in heaven. Give us this day our daily bread: and forgive us our trespasses, as we forgive them that trespass against us. And lead us not into temptation. But deliver us from evil.

11q: GS, pl. 17+.

Like the Sanctus melodies, those for the Agnus Dei ranged from moderately elaborate, for use on major feast days, to simple, for everyday use.
TRANSLATION
O Lamb of God, that takest away the sins of the world, have mercy upon us.
O Lamb of God, that takest away the sins of the world, have mercy upon us.
O Lamb of God, that takest away the sins of the world, grant us Thy peace.

11r: GS, pl. 117–118.

See note 11a. The text is paraphrased from the Epistle for the day.
TRANSLATION
Christ our Passover is sacrificed, alleluia: therefore let us keep the feast with the unleavened bread of sincerity and truth, alleluia, alleluia, alleluia.

11s: US, II, p. lxxvj.

The Postcommunion was recited to the same tone as the Collect. The number of Postcommunions recited corresponded to the number of Collects.
TRANSLATION
Pour into us, O Lord, the spirit of Thy love: that those whom Thou hast satisfied with the Paschal Sacrament, may of Thy goodness be made of one mind. Through Jesus Christ our Lord, who with Thee and the Holy Ghost liveth and reigneth, ever one God, world without end. Amen.

11t: GS, pl. 19+.

Mass ended with *Ite, missa est*, or with *Benedicamus Domino* if the Gloria had not been included. When a troped Kyrie was sung the Ite missa est was sung to the melody of the first Christe.
TRANSLATION
Depart; the Mass is ended. Thanks be to God.

12. The Play of Herod

Liturgical drama Anonymous from the Fleury play-book, 12th century

Characters: Archangel; Angels; Shepherds; Two midwives; Three Magi; Armiger; Herod; Interpreters; Courtiers; Two Scribes; Herod's son.

Scene I: The Adoration of the Shepherds

1. Here begins the book of the representation of Herod. When Herod and the other participants are ready, let the Angel with the multitude [of Angels] appear on high. Seeing this, the Shepherds are afraid. Let the Angel greet them, the others remaining silent:

No - li - te - ti - me - re vos, ec - ce e - nim e - van - ge - li - zo vo - bis gau - di - um

ma - gnum quod e - rit om - ni__ po - pu - lo; qui - a na - tus__ est no - - bis ho - di - e

Sal - va - - tor mun - di in ci - - vi - ta - te Da - vid,__ et__ hoc__ vo - bis__

si - gnum: In - ve - ni - e - tis in - fan - - tem pan - nis__ in - vo - lu - tum et__ po - si -

-tum__ in prae - se - pi - o in__ me - di - o du - um__ a - ni - ma - li - - um.__

2. And let the whole multitude suddenly say with the Angel:

Glo - ri - a in ex - cel - sis De - o.__ Et in ter - ra__ pax ho - mi - ni - bus bo - nae vo -

-lun - ta - tis. Al - le - lu - ia, al - le - lu - ia.

3. Then let the Shepherds, rising, sing among themselves:

Trans - e - a - mus__ us - que__ Beth - le - em, et__ vi - de - a - mus__ hoc__ ver -

-bum quod fa - ctum__ est, quod__ fe - cit Do - mi - nus et__ o - sten - dit__ no - bis.

4. Thus let them approach the manger, which has been prepared at the monastery doors. Then let two women guarding the manger question the Shepherds, saying:

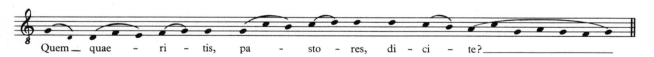

Quem__ quae - ri - tis, pa - sto - res, di - ci - te?__

5. Let the Shepherds reply:

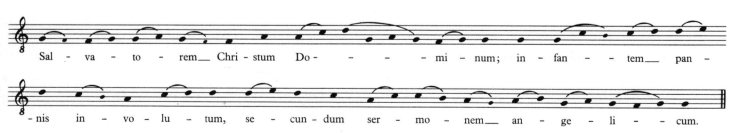

Sal - va - to - rem__ Chri - stum Do - - - - mi - num; in - fan - - tem__ pan -

-nis in - vo - lu - tum, se - cun - dum ser - mo - nem__ an - ge - li - - cum.

6. The Women:

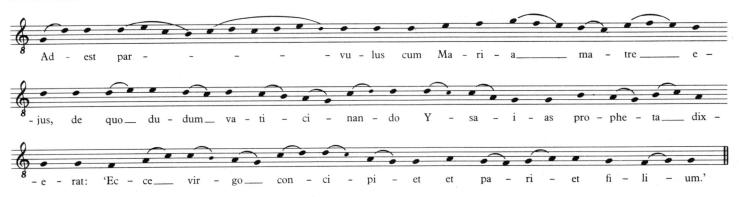

Ad - est par - - - - - vu - lus cum Ma - ri - a___ ma - tre___ e -

-jus, de quo__ du - dum__ va - ti - ci - nan - do Y - sa - i - as pro - phe - ta__ dix -

-e - rat: 'Ec - ce__ vir - go__ con - ci - pi - et et pa - ri - et fi - li - um.'

7. Then left the Shepherds, prostrating themselves, worship the Child, saying:

Sal - ve, Rex sae - cu - lo - rum.

8. Afterwards rising, let them invite the people standing around to worship the Child, saying to the crowd:

Ve - ni - te,___ ve - ni - te,___ ve - ni - te___ a - do - re - mus De - um, qui - a i - pse___

est___ Sal - va - tor no - ster.

Scene II: The Journey of the Magi

9. Meanwhile, let the Magi approach, each from his own corner as if from his own country; let them meet before the altar or by the Star, and while they approach let the first say:

Stel - - la ful - go - re ni - mi - o ru - ti - lat!

10. The second:

Quem ven - tu - rum o - - lim pro - phe - ta___ si - gna - ve - rat.

11. Then, standing side by side, let the one on the right say to the one in the middle:

Pax_____ ti - bi,___ fra - ter!

12. And let the latter reply:

Pax quo - que ti – bi!

13. Then let them kiss each other thus: the one in the middle and the one on the left: and the one on the left and the one on the right – a greeting for each one. Then let them show the Star to each other.

(First) Ec – ce stel – la! (Second) Ec – ce stel – la! (Third) Ec – ce stel – la!_____

14. Following the Star as it proceeds, let them say:

E – a – mus er – go et in – qui – ra – mus e – um, of – fe – ren – tes___ e – – i

mu – ne – ra:___ au – rum,___ thus_____ et___ myr – – rham. Qui – a___ Scri – ptum___

di – di – ci – mus: 'A – do – ra – bunt e – um om – nes re – ges, om – nes gen – tes ser – vi – ent e – – i.'

15. Coming to the quire door, let them question those standing there:

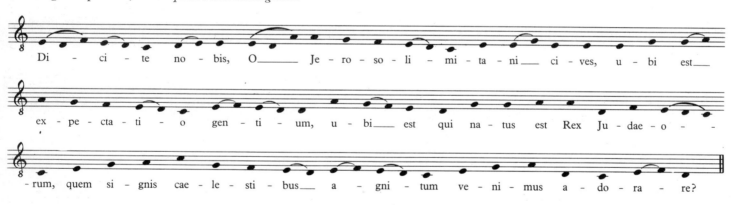

Di – ci – te no – bis, O___ Je – ro – so – li – mi – ta – ni___ ci – ves, u – bi est___

ex – pe – cta – ti – o gen – ti – um, u – bi___ est qui na – tus est Rex Ju – dae – o – –

-rum, quem si – gnis cae – le – sti – bus___ a – gni – tum ve – ni – mus a – do – ra – re?

Scene III: Herod's Court

16. Seeing the Magi, let Herod send his Armiger to them, the Armiger saying:

Quae___ re – rum_____ no – vi – tas, aut quae___ cau – sa sub – e – git___ vos i –

- gno – tas tem – pta – re___ vi – as? Quo ten – di – tis___ er – go? Quod ge –

- nus? Un – – de___ do – mo? Pa – – – cem ne huc fer – tis an___ ar – ma?

17. The reply of the Magi:

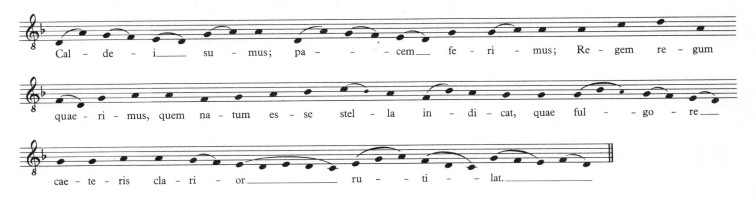

Cal - de - i su - mus; pa - - cem fe - ri - mus; Re - gem re - gum
quae - ri - mus, quem na - tum es - se stel - la in - di - cat, quae ful - - go - re
cae - te - ris cla - ri - or ru - ti - lat.

18. Having returned, let the Armiger salute the King; on bended knee let him say:

Vi - vat Rex in ae - ter - num!

19. Herod:

Sal - vet te gra - ti - a me - a!

20. The Armiger to the King:

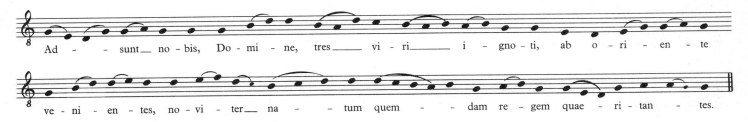

Ad - - sunt no - bis, Do - mi - ne, tres vi - ri i - gno - ti, ab o - ri - en - te
ve - ni - en - tes, no - vi - ter na - - tum quem - - dam re - gem quae - ri - tan - tes.

21. Then let Herod send his Messengers or Interpreters to the Magi, himself saying:

Lae - ti in - qui - si - to - res, qui sunt in - qui - ri - te re -
- ges, af - fo - re quos no - stris jam fa - ma re - vol - vit in o - ris.

22. The Interpreters to the Magi:

Prin - ci - pis e - di - ctu, re - ges, prae - sci - re ve - ni - mus quo sit pro -
- fe - - ctus hic ve - ster et un - de pro - fe - ctus.

23. The Magi:

Re - gem quae - si - tum du - ce stel - la si - gni - fi - ca - tum; mu -

-ne - re pro - vi - so pro - pe - ra - mus e - um___ ve - ne - ran - do.

24. The Interpreters, having returned to Herod:

Re - ges___ sunt___ A - ra - bum, cum tri - no___ mu - ne - re;___ na -

-tum quae - runt in - fan - tem, quem___ mon - strant si - de - ra Re - gem.

25. Herod, sending his Armiger to fetch the Magi:

An - te ve - ni - re___ ju - be, quo pos - sim sin - gu - la___ sci - re qui

sunt,___ cur___ ve - ni - ant, quo___ nos ru - mo - re___ re - qui - rant.

26. The Armiger [to Herod]

Quod man - das, ci - ti - us, Rex in - cli - te,___ per - fi - ci - e - tur.

27. The Armiger to the Magi:

Re - gi - a vos man - da - ta___ vo - cant; non se - gni - ter___ i - te.

28. The Armiger, leading the Magi to Herod:

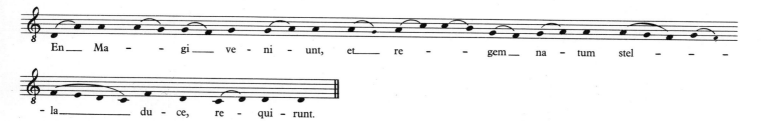

En Ma - gi ve - ni - unt, et___ re - gem___ na - tum stel -

- la___ du - ce, re - qui - runt.

29. Herod to the Magi:

Quae___ sit___ cau - sa___ vi - ae? Qui___ vos, vel___ un - de___

ve - ni - tis? Di - ci - te!

30. The Magi:

Rex___ est___ cau - sa - vi - ae; re - ges___ su - mus ex A - ra -

-bi - tis huc___ ve - ni - en - tes. Quae - ri - mus en___ Re - gem re - gnan - ti - bus im - pe - ri -

-tan - tem, Quem na - tum___ mun - do la - ctat Ju - da - i - ca vir - - - - go.

31. Herod to the Magi:

Re - gem, quem quae - ri - tis, na - tum es - se quo si - gno di - di - ci - stis?

32. The Magi:

Il - lum na - tum___ es - se di - di - ci - mus in O - ri - en - te, stel - la___ mon - stran - te.

33. Herod:

Si___ il - lum re - gna - re___ cre - di - tis?___ Di - ci - te no - bis!

34. The Magi:

Il - lum___ re - gna - re fa - ten - tes, cum my - sti - cis mu - ne - ri - bus de ter - ra___ lon - gin - qua

a - do - ra - re___ ve - ni - mus, tri - num___ De - um ve - ne - ran - tes tri - bus - cum mu - ne - ri - bus.___

35. And let them show the gifts.

Let the first Magus say: *The second:*   *The third:*

Au - ro re - gem.___   Thu - re De - um.   Myr - rha___ mor - ta - lem.

36. Then, let Herod order the Courtiers, who sit near him dressed as young men, to fetch the Scribes, who, bearded, sit nearby:

Vos___ me - i sy - my - stae, le - - - gis___ pe - ri - tos a - sci - te ut di -

- scant in Pro - phe - tis quid sen - ti - ant___ ex___ his.___

37. Let the Courtiers say to the Scribes, who bring with them the books of the Prophets:.

Vos, le - gis pe - ri - ti ad___ re - gem vo - ca - ti, cum Pro - phe - ta - rum___

li - bris pro - pe - ran - do ve - ni - te!

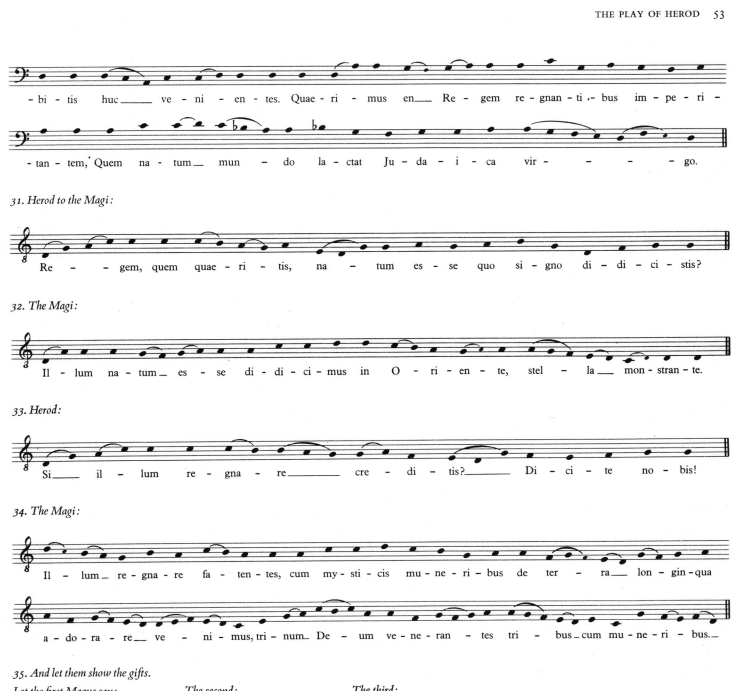

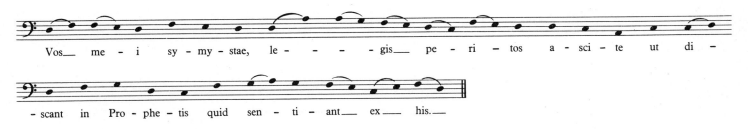

38. Afterwards let Herod question the Scribes, saying:

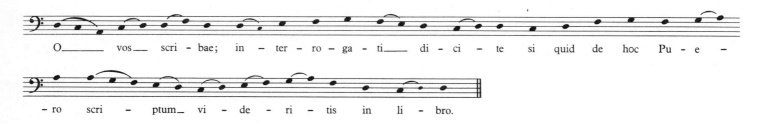

O vos scri - bae; in - ter - ro - ga - ti di - ci - te si quid de hoc Pu - e -

- ro scri - ptum vi - de - ri - tis in li - bro.

39. Then let two Scribes turn the pages of the book and at length, as if having found the prophecy, let them say:

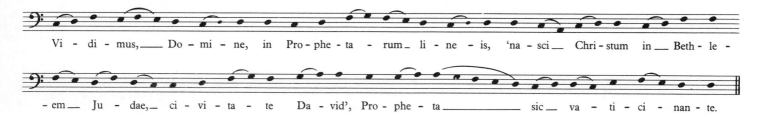

Vi - di - mus, Do - mi - ne, in Pro - phe - ta - rum li - ne - is, 'na - sci Chri - stum in Beth - le -

- em Ju - dae, ci - vi - ta - te Da - vid', Pro - phe - ta sic va - ti - ci - nan - te.

40. And, showing the place with a finger, let them hand the book to the unbelieving King, [saying]:

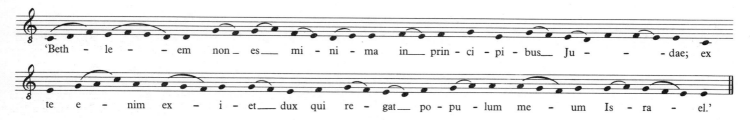

'Beth - le - em non es mi - ni - ma in prin - ci - pi - bus Ju - dae; ex

te e - nim ex - i - et dux qui re - gat po - pu - lum me - um Is - ra - el.'

41. Then let Herod, seeing the prophecy and being filled with rage, throw down the book; but let his son, hearing the noise, go to soothe his father, and standing before him let him say:

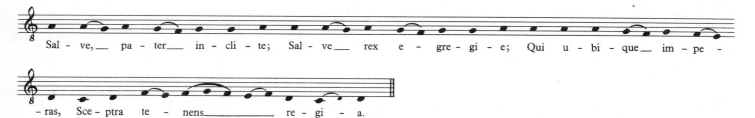

Sal - ve, pa - ter in - cli - te; Sal - ve rex e - gre - gi - e; Qui u - bi - que im - pe -

- ras, Sce - ptra te - nens re - gi - a.

42. Herod:

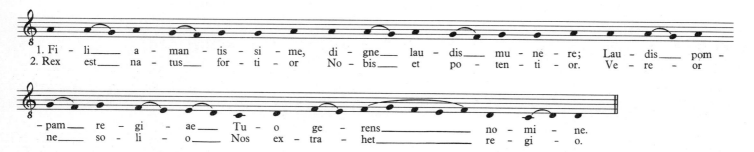

1. Fi - li a - man - tis - si - me, di - gne lau - dis mu - ne - re; Lau - dis pom -
2. Rex est na - tus for - ti - or No - bis et po - ten - ti - or. Ve - re - or

- pam re - gi - ae Tu - o ge - rens no - mi - ne.
ne so - li - o Nos ex - tra - het re - gi - o.

43. Then let the son, speaking lightly of Christ, offer himself as a defender, saying:

Con - tra il - lum re - gu - lum, Con - tra na - tum par - vu - lum, Ju - be,

pa - ter, fi - li - um Hoc in - i - re proe - li - um.

44. Then at length let Herod send away the Magi to seek the Child, having made homage before them to the newborn King, saying:

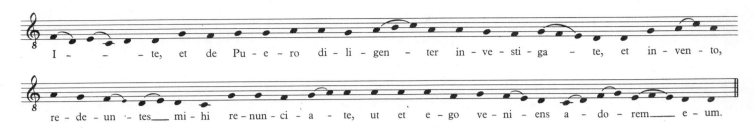

I — — te, et de Pu — e — ro di — li — gen — ter in — ve — sti — ga — te, et in — ven — to,

re — de — un — tes___ mi — hi re — nun — ci — a — te, ut et e — go ve — ni — ens a — do — rem___ e — um.

As the Magi depart, let the Star, not yet noticed by Herod, precede them. Let them point it out to each other. When Herod and his son see it, let them threaten it with their swords.

Scene IV: The Adoration of the Magi

45. The Magi:

Ec — ce stel — la in O — ri — en — te___ prae — vi — sa i — te — rum prae — ce — dit nos lu — ci — da.

46. Meanwhile let the Shepherds, returning from the manger, come with rejoicing and singing:

O___ re — gem cae — — li,___ cu — i___ ta — li — a___ fa — mu — lan —

— tur___ ob — — se — qui — a!___ Sta — bu — lo___ po — — ni — — tur___

___ qui con — ti — net___ mun — — — — dum.___ Ja — cet in___ prae — se — —

— pi — o,___ et in nu — — bi — bus___ to — — nat.___

47. The Magi to the Shepherds:

Quem vi — di — stis?___

48. The Shepherds:

Se — cun — dum___ quod di — ctum est no — bis ab An — ge — lo___ de Pu — e —

— ro i — sto,___ in — ve — ni — mus in — fan — tem pan — — nis in — vo — lu — tum et___ po — si —

— tum___ in prae — se — pi — o___ in___ me — di — o du — um___ a — ni — ma — li — — um.___

49. After the Shepherds have gone, let the Magi follow the Star as far as the manger, saying:

Quem non prae — va — lent pro — pri — a ma — gni — tu — di — ne cae — lum, ter — ra at — que ma — ri — a la — ta ca —

-pe - re, De vir - gi - ne - o na - tus u - te - ro; po - ni - tur in prae - se - pi - o. Ser - mo ce - ci - nit

quem va - ti - di - cus stant si - mul bos et a - si - nus. Sed o - ri - tur stel - la lu - ci - da, prae - bi - tum

Do - mi - no ob - se - qui - a. Quem Ba - la - am ex Ju - da - i - ca na - sci - tu - rum dix - e - rat pro - sa -

- pi - a. Haec no - stro - rum o - cu - los ful - gu - ran - ti lu - mi - ne prae - strinx - it lu - ci - da. Et nos

i - psos pro - vi - de du - cens ad cu - na - bu - la re - splen - dens ful - gi - da.

50. *Then let the Midwives, seeing the Magi, say among themselves:*

Qui sunt hii qui, stel - la du - ce, nos ad - e - un - tes in - au - di - ta fe - runt?

51. *The Magi:*

Nos su - mus quos cer - ni - tis, re - ges Thar - sis et A - ra - bum et Sa - bae, do - na fe - ren -

- tes Chri - sto na - to, Re - gi, Do - mi - no, quem stel - la du - cen - te, a - do - ra - re ve - ni - mus.

52. *The Midwives, showing the Child:*

Ec - ce pu - er ad - est quem quae - ri - tis. Jam pro - pe - ra - te et a - do - ra - te, qui - a

i - pse est re - dem - pti - o mun - di.

53. *The Magi:* [*First*]   [*Second*]   [*Third*]

Sal - ve, Rex sae - cu - lo - rum!   Sal - ve, De - us de - o - rum!   Sal - ve, sa - lus mor - tu - o - rum.

54. *Then let the Magi prostrate themselves and worship the child and make their offerings:*

[*The first Magus*]   [*The second*]

Su - sci - pe, Rex, au - rum, Re - gis si - gnum.   Su - sci - pe myr - rham,

[*The third*]

si - gnum se - pul - tu - rae.   Su - sci - pe thus, tu ve - re De - us.

55. *This done, let the Magi begin to sleep before the manger; then let an Angel appear above them and warn them in their sleep to return to their own lands by another road. Let the Angel say:*

Im - ple - ta sunt om - ni - a quae pro - phe - ti - ce scri - pta____ sunt. I - te, vi - am__ re - me -

-an - tes__ a - li - am, nec de - la - to - - res tan - ti re - gis pu - ni - en - di_____ e - ri - tis.

56. *The Magi, awaking:*

De - o gra - ti - as. Sur - ga - mus er - go, vi - si - o - ne mo - ni - ti an - ge - li - ca, et,____

cal - le mu - ta - to, la - te - ant He - - ro - dem quae vi - di - mus_ de_____ Pu - e - ro.

57. *Then let the Magi, returning by another route and not being seen by Herod, say:*

O_____ ad - mi - ra - bi - le com - mer - ci - um! Cre - a - tor ge - ne - ris hu - ma - ni, a - ni -

-ma - - tum cor - pus su - mens, de Vir - gi - ne na - sci di - gna - - tus_ est: et pro - ce -

-dens ho - mo si - ne_____ se - mi - ne, lar - gi - tus est no - bis su - am__ de - i - ta - tem.

58. *Then, [the Magi] coming into the quire, saying:*

Gau - - de - te, fra - tres,_ Chri - stus no - bis_ na - tus_____ est; De - us ho - mo_ fa - ctus_ est.

59. *Then the Precentor begins:*

[Choir]

Te De - um lau - da - mus:_ *te Do - mi - num con - fi - te - mur. Te__ ae - ter - num Pa -

-trem om - nis_ ter - ra ve - ne - ra - tur. Ti - bi om - nes An - ge - li, ti - bi__ Cae - li et

u - ni - ver - sae Po - te - sta - tes: Ti - bi Che - ru - bim et Se - ra - phim in - ces - sa - bi - li

vo - ce pro - cla - mant: San - - ctus:_ San - - ctus:_ San - - ctus_ Do - mi - nus

De - us__ Sa - ba - oth. Ple - ni sunt cae - li et ter - ra ma - je - sta - tis glo - ri - ae__ tu -

-sto - di - re. Mi - se - re - re no - stri Do - mi - ne, mi - se - re - re no - stri. Fi - at mi -

-se - ri - cor - di - a tu - a Do - mi - ne su - per nos, quem - ad - mo - dum spe - ra - vi - mus in te.

In te Do - mi - ne spe - ra - vi: non con - fun - dar in ae - ter - num.

Thus it ends.

Orléans, Bibliothèque de la Ville, MS 201, ff. 205–20.

The origin of *liturgical drama* has been traced to the addition of a trope in dialogue form, beginning 'Quem quaeritis', attached to the Introit of Mass on Easter Day in a 10th-century manuscript. Subsequently this dialogue was transferred from Mass to the end of Matins, a position which allowed it to expand and include other events on Easter Day. During the 11th century certain other subjects, such as the visits of the shepherds and the magi to the manger, came to be treated in a similar fashion, as part of Matins on the appropriate day. More highly-developed and 'dramatic' representations, such as the present example, appeared in the 12th and 13th centuries, after which the genre gave way to the more theatrical mystery plays, staged outside the church. The *Play of Herod* is a particularly sophisticated example of liturgical drama, developing its characters quite thoroughly and having unusually full rubrics for performance. Some of its material comes straight from the liturgy while the remainder appears to be freshly composed. Its place within Matins is indicated by the fact that it ends with the singing of the *Te Deum*, sung at the end of Matins on occasions of special solemnity. (For another view of the origin of liturgical drama, see Timothy McGee, 'The liturgical placements of the *Quem quaeritis* dialogue', in *Journal of the American Musicological Society*, Spring 1976.)

NOTES AND TRANSLATION

1: This and the following number are non-liturgical settings of Gospel texts.
Be frightened no longer! For behold, I bring you good tidings of great joy which shall be to all people; for unto us is born this day in the city of David a Saviour of the world, and this shall be a sign for you: You shall find the Child wrapped in swaddling clothes and lying in a manger between two beasts.

2: See note 1.
Glory to God in the highest, and on earth peace towards men of good will; alleluia, alleluia.

3: An antiphon borrowed from the liturgy.
Let us go unto Bethlehem, and see this Word which is come to pass, which the Lord has done and made known to us.

4–6: A dialogue taken from the trope of the Introit for the third Mass of Christmas.
Whom do you seek, O shepherds? Tell us.
The Saviour, Jesus Christ, the Lord; the Infant, wrapped in swaddling clothes, according to the words of the angel.
The Child is here with Mary His mother; Isaiah the prophet foretold His coming in days long past: 'Behold, a virgin shall conceive and bear a son.'

7: Hail, King for all time!

8: Come, come, come, let us worship God, for He alone is our Saviour.

9: The changes of scene are not specified in the MS.
The star shines with great brightness!

10: Of whose coming the prophet spoke in days past.

11: Peace be with you, brother!

12: Peace be also with you!

13: Behold the star!

14: Let us go therefore and seek Him, offering Him gifts: gold, frankincense and myrrh. For we know the Scripture 'All Kings shall worship Him, all people shall serve Him.'

15: Tell us, O citizens of Jerusalem, where is He, expected by the people? Where is He who is born King of the Jews, whom, revealed by signs from heaven, we have come to worship?

16: What novelty or cause prompted you to attempt an unknown journey? Where are you going? Of what race are you? Where is your home? Do you bring peace or war?

17: We are Chaldaeans; we bring peace. We seek the King of kings, whose birth the star reveals, shining more brightly than the other stars.

18: O king, live for ever!

19: Greetings to you and my thanks!

20: Lord, three unknown men are with us, coming from the East, seeking a King who is newly born.

21: Joyful messengers, ask these kings who they are; question them concerning Him whose fame is already circulating.

22: By the command of the prince, O kings, we have come to discover why you have made your journey here and whence you have come.

23: Led by the sign from a star, we seek a King who is promised; provided with gifts we hasten to worship Him.

24: They are kings of Arabia, bearing gifts, seeking a new-born Infant, whom the stars reveal as a King.

25: Order them to come before me so that I may know these things: who they are, why they come, what rumour brings them to us.

26: What you command, O illustrious king, shall quickly be done.

27: The royal commands summon you; come without delay.

28: Behold, the Magi are coming. And, led by a star, they seek a new-born King.

29: What is the reason for your journey? Who are you? Whence do you come? Answer!

30: A King is the reason for our journey. We are kings, coming hither from Arabia. Behold, we seek a King who rules all other rulers, who, born without sin, is suckled by a Jewish maiden.

31: By what sign did you learn that the King whom you seek had been born?

32: We learnt in the East that He had been born, the star showing us.

33: If you believe that He reigns, tell us!

34: Acknowledging that He reigns, we have come with mystic gifts from distant lands to worship Him, paying tribute with three gifts to the God who is three in one.

35: Gold for a king. Incense for a God. Myrrh for a mortal.

36: You, my courtiers, summon those skilled in the law, that they may say what they find in the prophets concerning this.

37: You, skilled in the law and summoned to the king, come in haste with the books of the prophets!

38: O you scribes, say if you see anything concerning this Boy written in the book.

39: We have seen, O Lord, in the sayings of the prophets: 'Christ is born in Bethlehem of Judaea, in the city of David.' Thus the prophet has foretold.

40: This incipit has been completed from Madrid, Biblioteca Nacional, MS 289, f. 109v.
'Thou, Bethlehem, art not the least among the princes of Judah; for out of thee shall come a governor that shall rule my people Israel.'

41: Hail, illustrious father; hail, admirable king, who rules everywhere, holding your royal sceptre.

42: Beloved son, worthy of your share of praise, carrying in your name the dignity of kingship: a King is born, stronger and more powerful than us. I fear that He will drag us from our throne.

43: Father, order your son that battle be commenced against that petty King, against that new-born paltry Child.

44: Go and search diligently for the Boy, and, having found Him, bring word to me so that I may come to worship Him.

45: Behold, the star already seen in the East still goes glittering before us.

46: The incipit of this responsory has been completed from AS, pl. 78.
O King of Heaven, whom all serve in obedience! He who unites the world is placed in a stable; He lies in a manger, and thunders in the clouds.

47: Whom have you seen?

48: According to what was told us by the angel concerning this Child, we found the Infant wrapped in swaddling clothes and placed in a manger between two beasts.

49: This text is borrowed from a Sequence but does not employ the usual melody.
He whom the vastness of heaven and earth cannot surpass or the wide seas contain, is born of a virgin womb; He is laid in a manger; as the prophet foretold in a prophecy, an ox and an ass stand with Him. But the shining star rises, paying its homage to Him whom Balaam prophesied would be born of the Jewish race. This Star has blinded our eyes with the brilliance of its light, providentially leading us to the cradle with its majestic brightness.

50: Who are these, coming towards us, who, led by the star, carry strange burdens?

51: We whom you see are kings of Tarsus and the Arabs and of Saba, bearing gifts for the new-born Christ, the King, the Lord.

52: Behold, here is the Child whom you seek. Now hurry and adore Him, for He is the Saviour of the world.

53: Hail, King of the ages! Hail, God of gods! Hail, Saviour of the dead!

54: Accept, O King, gold, the emblem of a king. Accept myrrh, the emblem of the grave. Accept incense, thou true God.

55: All things are fulfilled that were written in prophecy. Go, take another way home, so that you will not betray to punishment so great a King.

56: Thanks be to God. Warned by the angelic vision, let us therefore rise and, changing our route, let them conceal from Herod what we have seen concerning the Child.

57: The incipit of this antiphon has been completed from LU, pp. 442–3.
O wonderful compact! The Creator of the human race, assuming a living body, deigned to be born of a virgin, and, becoming man without earthly seed, gave to us His own divinity.

58: Rejoice, brothers. Christ is born for us. God is made man.

59: The incipit of this ancient hymn, with which Matins ended on the most important feasts, has been completed from LU, pp. 1832–4.
We praise Thee, O God: we acknowledge Thee to be the Lord. All the earth doth worship Thee: the Father everlasting. To Thee all Angels cry aloud: the heavens and all the powers therein. To Thee Cherubim and Seraphim: continually do cry, Holy, Holy, Holy: Lord God of Sabaoth; Heaven and earth are full of the Majesty: of Thy glory. The glorious company of the Apostles praise Thee. The goodly fellowship of the Prophets praise Thee. The noble army of Martyrs praise Thee. The holy Church throughout all the world doth acknowledge Thee. The Father of an infinite Majesty; Thine honourable, true and only Son; Also the Holy Ghost, the Comforter. Thou art the King of glory, O Christ. Thou art the everlasting Son of the Father. When Thou tookest upon Thee to deliver man Thou didst not abhor the Virgin's womb. When Thou hadst overcome the sharpness of death Thou didst open the kingdom of heaven to all believers. Thou sittest at the right hand of God in the glory of the Father. We believe that Thou shalt come to be our Judge. We therefore pray Thee, help Thy servants, whom Thou hast redeemed with Thy precious blood. Make them to be numbered with Thy Saints in Glory everlasting. O Lord, save Thy people and bless Thine heritage. Govern them and lift them up for ever. Day by day we magnify Thee; And we worship Thy Name ever world without end. Vouchsafe, O Lord, to keep us this day without sin. O Lord, have mercy upon us; have mercy upon us. O Lord, let Thy mercy lighten upon us as our trust is in Thee. O Lord, in Thee have I trusted; let me never be confounded.

Secular Monophony

13. Mors vite propitia

Conductus Anonymous (French, c.1200)

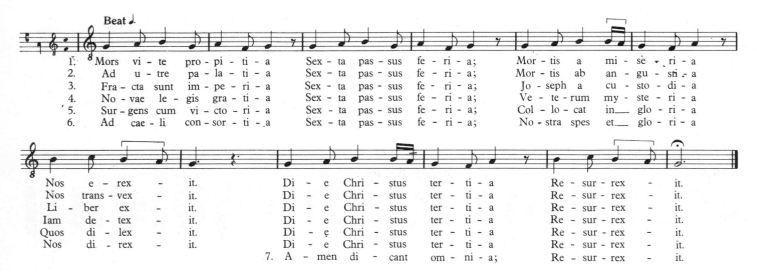

Florence, Biblioteca Medicea-Laurenziana, MS Pluteus 29.1, f.464r.

During the 12th century there arose in France a type of rhymed, metrical, and usually strophic Latin poem known as the *conductus*. Conductus texts were serious in tone, being concerned with devotional, moral, topical, and political subjects. Though non-liturgical they were sometimes sung in church services as an additional item or as a substitute for the *Benedicamus Domino*. Conductus formed a major part of the Notre Dame repertory, disappearing in the later 13th century as composers concentrated upon the *motet*. Polyphonic examples are given as Nos. 51–55.

TRANSLATION

Death, the propitiation of our life, He suffered on the sixth day, He raised us from the misery of death. On the third day Christ rose again. To another mansion, suffering . . ., He conveyed us from the straits of death. On . . .

Empires are broken, suffering . . ., Joseph escaped free from the search-party. On . . .

By the grace of the new law, suffering . . ., He now laid bare the mysteries of the Ancients. On . . .

Ascending with victory, suffering . . ., He leads into glory those whom He loved. On . . .

To the delights of heaven, suffering . . ., our hope and glory, He led us. On . . .

Let all things say 'Amen': He is risen.

14. Can vei la lauzeta mover

Canso in vers form Bernart de Ventadorn (c.1125–c.1180)

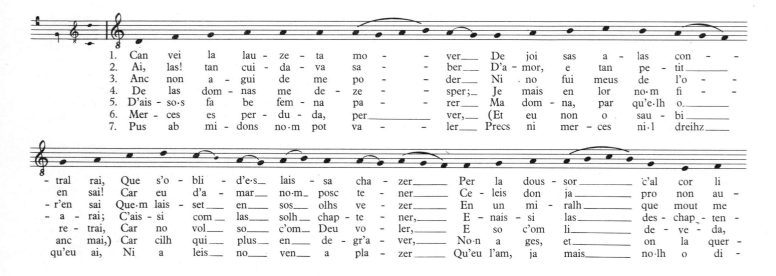

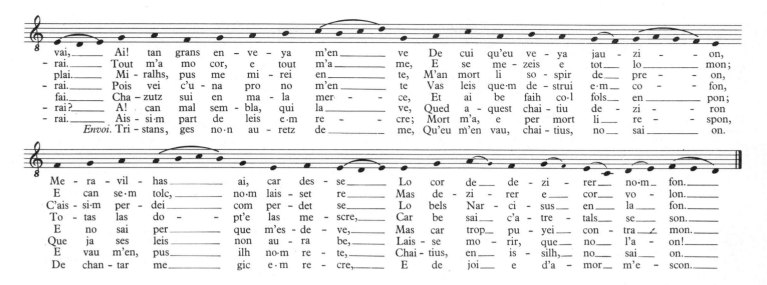

vai,_____ Ai! tan grans en - ve - ya m'en _____ ve De cui qu'eu ve - ya jau - zi - ___ on,
- rai._____ Tout m'a mo cor, e tout m'a _____ me, E se me - zeis e tot __ lo ___ mon;
plai._____ Mi - ralhs, pus me mi - rei en _____ te, M'an mort li so - spir de __ pre - __ on,
- rai._____ Pois vei c'u - na pro no m'en _____ te Vas leis que·m de - strui e·m __ co - __ fon,
fai._____ Cha - zutz sui en ma la mer _____ ce, Et ai be faih co·l fols __ en __ pon;
- rai? A! can mal sem - bla, qui la _____ ve, Qued a - quest chai - tiu de - zi - __ ron
- rai._____ Ais - si·m part de leis e·m re - __ cre; Mort m'a, e per mort li re - __ spon,
Envoi. Tri - stans, ges no·n au - retz de _____ me, Qu'eu m'en vau, chai - tius, no __ sai __ on.

Me - ra - vil - has _____ ai, car des - se _____ Lo cor de __ de - zi - rer no·m fon. _____
E can se·m tolc, _____ no·m lais - set re _____ Mas de - zi - rer e __ cor vo - lon.
C'ais - si·m per - dei _____ com per - det se _____ Lo bels Nar - ci - sus __ en __ la __ fon.
To - tas las do - __ pt'e las me - scre, _____ Car be sai __ c'a - tre - tals se __ son.
E no sai per _____ que m'es - de - ve, _____ Mas car trop __ pu - yei con - tra __ mon.
Que ja ses leis _____ non au - ra be, _____ Lais - se mo - rir, que no l'a - on!
E vau m'en, pus _____ ilh no·m re - te, _____ Chai - tius, en is - silh, no __ sai __ on.
De chan - tar me _____ gic e·m re - cre, _____ E de joi e d'a - mor __ m'e - scon. _____

Paris, Bibliothèque National, MS. fr. 22543, f. 56.
H. van der Werf, *The Chansons of the Troubadours and Trouvères* (Utrecht, 1972), pp. 93–95.

For the area of southern France known as Provence the 12th century was a period of considerable prosperity, encouraging many kinds of cultural achievement. The tropes, sequences, and polyphony of the 'St Martial school' demonstrate the flourishing condition of church music. Poetry in the vernacular was produced in large quantities and was associated for the first time with a melodic repertory whose function was definitely secular. The poets who wrote in Provençal (also called the *langue d'oc*) were known as *trobadors*. Many of them were aristocrats – members of a feudal élite who, in a time of relative stability, were able to cultivate artistic pursuits. Others, such as the author of this example, were of humbler birth. The trobador movement was virtually extinguished with the reduction of Provence by the French monarchy in the 12th and early 13th centuries.

One of the favourite themes of the trobadors was that of courtly love, or *amor cortois*, in which the lover was purified by experiencing an undeclared and unconsummated love for the beloved, who was unattainable in her perfection. Poems dealing with the theme of amor cortois were known as *canso*. Poems on other topics were known by other names; they included the *alba*, in which lovers were warned of the approach of day (see No. 20); the *sirventes*, a serious discussion of a moral, political, or other abstract topic (see No. 25); the *planh*, a lament (see No. 15); the *pastoral*, a poem with an outdoor, rural setting (see No. 18); the *tenso*, a debate between two or more characters (see No. 26); and the *crusade song* (see No. 19). These various genres are distinguished from each other by their subject matter, not by any inherent differences in poetical or musical form.

Although only about one tenth of trobador poems survive with melodies, it would seem that they were usually sung, or possibly sometimes declaimed to an improvised instrumental accompaniment. The extent of the musical contribution of the trobadors themselves is not known. Some of them probably employed professional musicians or entertainers to furnish their poems with melodies, while others may have made up their own tunes. Trobador melodies vary considerably in character. Some are strikingly elaborate and melismatic; others are extremely simple and syllabic. Some (known as *vers*) make no use of melodic repetition; others use melodic repetition in various ways. In view of the intensive cultivation of sacred music in Provence it is not surprising that some trobador melodies show characteristics of plainsong. The present example, a *vers*, shows plainsong influence in its predominantly stepwise motion and in the suggestion of a 'tenor' or reciting note in the first line. The notation of trobador melodies does not indicate rhythm. We have transcribed most of our examples as if they had been plainsong. We would emphasize that definitively 'correct' transcriptions of this repertory are unattainable; too little evidence survives concerning the way in which the trobador repertory was sung, and there is indeed no evidence that performance practice was consistent from one place to another. The reader is free to apply rhythmic interpretation to these transcriptions and to add instrumental preludes, interludes, and postludes in any way which seems to him to be musically appropriate and effective.

TRANSLATION

When I see the lark beating its wings joyfully against the sun's rays, which then swoons and swoops down, because of the joy in its heart, oh! I feel such jealousy for all those who have the joy of love, that I am astonished that my heart does not immediately melt with desire! Alas! I thought I knew so much of love, and I know so little; for I cannot help loving a lady from whom I shall never obtain any favour. She has taken away my heart and myself, and herself and the whole world; and when she left me, I had nothing left but desire and a yearning heart.

I have no power over myself, and have not had possession of myself since the time when she allowed me to look into her eyes, in a mirror which I like very much. Mirror, since I was reflected in you, deep sighs have killed me, for I caused my own ruin, just as fair Narcissus caused his by looking in the fountain.

I despair of ladies; I shall not trust them ever again; just as I used to defend them, now I shall condemn them. Since I see that *one* of them does not help me against her who is ruining and destroying me I fear them all and have no faith in them, for I know they are all the same.

My lady shows herself to be [merely] a woman (and that is why I reproach her) in that she does not want what one should want, and she does what is forbidden her. I have fallen out of favour, and have acted like the fool on the bridge; and I do not know why this has happened to me, unless it was because I tried to climb too high.

Mercy is gone, that is sure, and I never received any of it, for she who should have the most mercy has none, and where else should I seek it? Oh! how difficult it is for a person who sees her to imagine that she would allow to die this poor yearning wretch, and would not help the man who can have no help but her!

Since pleas and mercy and my rights cannot help me to win my lady, and since it does not please her that I love her, I shall speak to her about it no more. So I am leaving her and her service; she has killed me, and I reply with death, and I am going sadly away, since she will not accept my service, into exile, I do not know where.

Tristan, you will hear no more of me, for I am going sadly away, I do not know where. I am going to stop singing, and I flee from love and joy.

15. Fortz chausa es

Planh in vers form (1199)   Gaulcem Faidit (*c.*1170–*c.*1205)

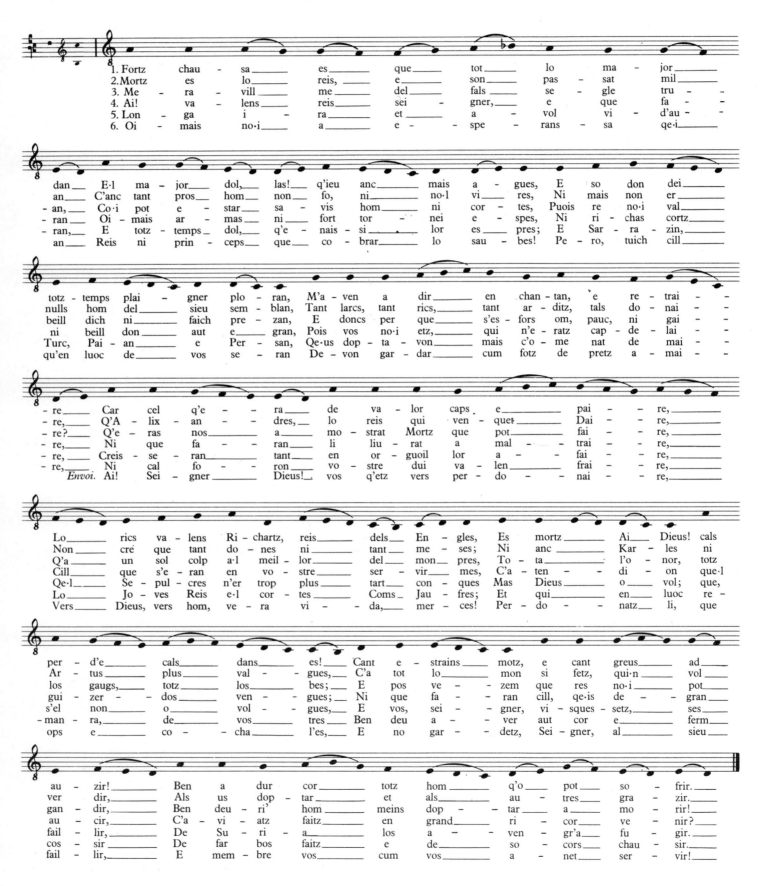

Paris, Bibliothèque National, MS fr. 20050, f. 87.
R. T. Hill and T. G. Bergin, *Anthology of the Provençal Troubadours*,
Vol. 1 (New Haven, 1973), pp. 130–1.

This planh, lamenting the death of the English king Richard I (d. 1199), is set to a *vers* or through-composed melody. Although no line of the melody is repeated exactly, restatement of two- and three-note cells does occur, giving the piece the character of a controlled improvisation.

TRANSLATION

It is a very grievous thing that I have to recount and tell in my song of the greatest loss and the greatest sorrow, alas! that I have ever experienced (and which I must for ever lament in tears) – for he who was the head and father of valour, the powerful and worthy Richard, king of England, is dead – Ah, God! what a loss and misfortune it is! What a cruel word and how terrible to hear! Hard indeed is the heart of him who can bear it.

The king is dead, and a thousand years have passed since there ever existed or was seen a man so valiant, and there never will be a man like him, so generous, so powerful, so daring, so liberal, that I doubt whether Alexander, the king who defeated Darius, gave or spent as much as he; and never did Charlemagne or Arthur have so much worth, for, to tell the truth, Richard made himself universally feared by some and loved by others.

I am amazed, considering the deceit and treachery of the age, how there can exist a wise and courtly man since now fine words and glorious exploits are worth nothing; and so why should a man strive either a little or a lot? For now Death has shown what it can do, that with one blow it took the best in the world along with all the honour, all the joys, all the benefits; and since we see that nothing can escape death we ought to fear it much less.

Ah! worthy Lord and King, what will now happen to arms and hard-fought tournaments, and rich courts and fine and magnificent gifts, since you, who were at the head, are no longer here? And what will now happen to those who had devoted themselves to your service and were waiting for their reward to come but are now thrown into misery? And what will happen to those whom you had raised to riches and power but who now should kill themselves?

Their lives will be wretched, full of endless grief and lasting sadness for that is their fate; and the Saracens, the Turks, the Pagans, and the Persians, who were afraid of you more than of any other man born of a mother, will advance their cause so arrogantly that the Sepulchre will not be conquered until much later – but this is God's will; for if he had not allowed this, and if you, my Lord, had lived, you would have certainly caused them to flee from Syria.

Henceforth there is no hope that any king or prince who could capture it will go there! However, all those who will take your place must consider how much you loved merit, and must remember what your two valiant brothers were like, the young king [Henry] and the courtly count Geoffrey [of Brittany]; and whoever remains in your place should have the qualities of you three: a high courage, and the firm resolve to perform good deeds and to offer help.

Ah! Lord God, you who forgive truly, true God, true man, true life, have mercy! Pardon him for his need is urgent and, Lord, do not look upon his sin but remember how he went to serve you!

16. Atressi com l'olifanz

Canso **Rigaut de Berbezilh** (*c.*1170–*c.*1210)

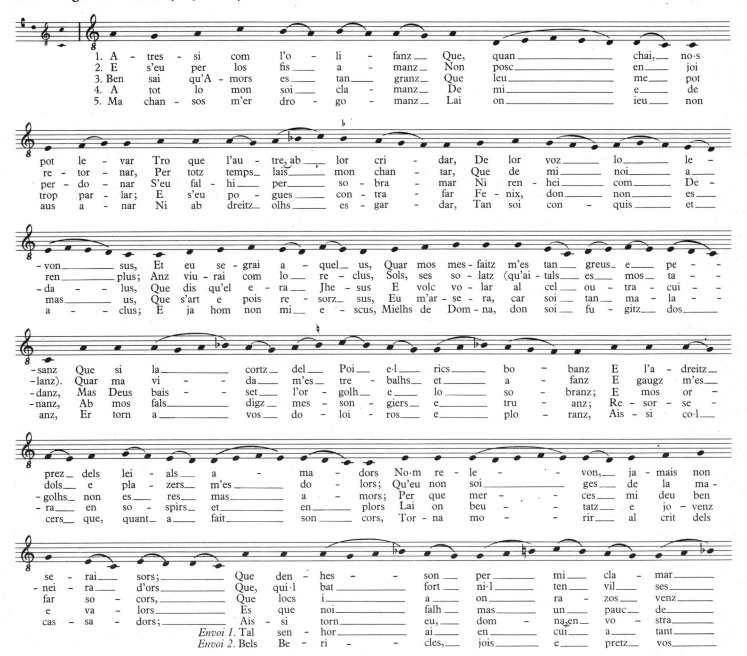

mer	–	ce	Lai	on	pre	jars	ni	ra	zos	no·m	val – re.
mer	–	ce,	El	en –	grais -	sa	e	mel	hu –	r'e	re – ve.
mer	–	ce	E	locs	on	dreitz	ni	ra –	zos	no	val – re.
mer	–	ce	Que	noi	si –	on	as -	sem	blat	tuit	li – be.
mer	–	ce;	Mas	vos	non	cal,	si	d'a –	mor,	no·us	so – ve.
de	–	be,	Quan	m'en	so –	ve	no	posc	fal –	hir	en – re.
man	–	te;	Tot	quant	volh	ai,	quan	de	vos	me	so – ve.

Paris, Bibliothèque National, MS fr. 20050, ff. 84r–v.
R. T. Hill and T. G. Bergin, *Anthology of the Provençal Troubadours*, Vol. 1 (New Haven, 1973), pp. 92–4.

Some repetition occurs in this unusually elaborate melody (compare line 6 with line 10, and line 7 with line 11). Rigaut was well known for poems based on an extravagant comparison such as begins the first stanza.

TRANSLATION

Just as the elephant which, when it falls, cannot get up again until the others, with the cries of their voices, set it on its feet again, so will I also follow this custom, for my misdeeds are so grievous and heavy for me to bear that, if the court of the Puy and the rich glory and worthy merit of true lovers do not raise me up, I never will be raised; may they deign on my behalf to beg for mercy where my prayers and arguments are ineffective.

And if I cannot return to a state of joy with the help of the true lovers, I abandon my singing for ever for there will be nothing more from me; but I shall live like a recluse, alone, without company (for such is my desire). For my life is a burden and a torment to me, and joy is sadness and pleasure is grief; for I am not like the bear which, even if it is beaten hard and mercilessly ill-treated, thrives, improves and is fully restored.

I am well aware that Love is so powerful that it can easily forgive me if I have sinned by loving to excess or have behaved like Daedalus who said that he was Jesus and wanted, in his presumption, to fly up to heaven but whose pride and arrogance were humbled by God; and my pride is nothing but love, which is why mercy must certainly come to my aid for there are occasions on which reason prevails over mercy and occasions where reason is worth nothing.

I am one who is pleading to everyone about myself and about my indiscretion; and if I could imitate the phoenix, this unique bird which burns itself and then rises again, I would burn myself for I am so wretched with my false, deceitful and perfidious words; I would rise again with sighs and tears where beauty, youth and valour are to be found, and where there is lacking only a modicum of pity for all good qualities to be gathered together.

My song will act as an interpreter for me where I dare not go and on whom I dare not gaze directly, so overcome and humbled am I; and let no one make excuses for me, my supreme lady, from whom I have fled these two years; now I return to you griefstricken and in tears, just like the hart which, having run its course, turns back at the cry of the hunters, only to die; so I return to your mercy, my lady; yet it means nothing to you if you do not recall our love.

I have such a lord in whom so much good exists that when I remember him I can fail in nothing.

Beautiful Beryl, may joy and worth keep you; I have all that I wish when I remember you.

17. Del sieu tort farai esmenda

Canso in vers form   **Peirol** (*c.*1160–*c.*1225)

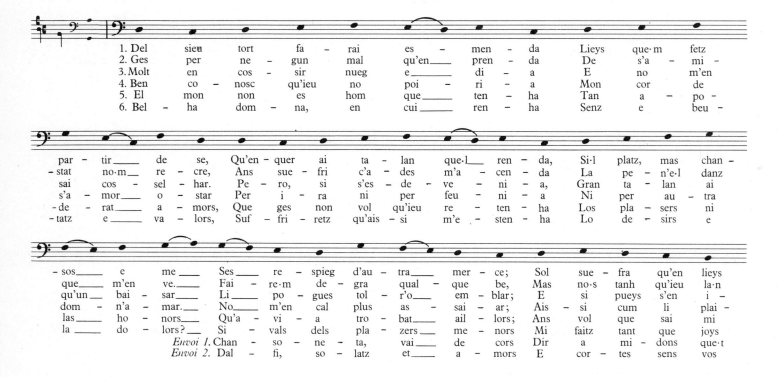

1. Del	sieu	tort	fa –	rai	es –	men –	da	Lieys	que·m	fetz
2. Ges	per	ne –	gun	mal	qu'en	pren –	da	De	s'a –	mi –
3. Molt	en	cos –	sir	nueg	e	di –	a	E	no	m'en
4. Ben	co –	nosc	qu'ieu	no	poi –	ri –	a	Mon	cor	de
5. El	mon	non	es	hom	que	ten –	ha	Tan	a –	po –
6. Bel –	ha	dom –	na,	en	cui	ren –	ha	Senz	e	beu –

par –	tir	de	se,	Qu'en – quer	ai	ta –	lan	que·l	ren –	da,	Si·l	platz,	mas	chan –
- stat	no·m	re –	cre,	Ans	sue – fri	c'a –	des	m'a –	cen –	da,	La	pe –	n'e·l	danz
sai	cos –	sel –	har.	Pe – ro,	si	s'es –	de –	ve –	ni –	a,	Gran	ta –	lan	ai
s'a –	mor	o –	star	Per	i – ra	ni	per	feu –	ni –	a,	Ni	per	au –	tra
- de –	rat	a –	mors,	Que	ges	non	vol	qu'ieu	re –	ten –	ha	Los	pla –	sers	ni
- tatz	e	va –	lors,	Suf – fri	retz	qu'ais –	si	m'e	sten –	ha	Lo	de –	sirs	e

- sos	e	me	Ses	re – spieg	d'au –	tra	mer –	ce;	Sol	sue – fra	qu'en	lieys
que	m'en	ve.	Fai –	re·m	de – gra	qual –	que	be,	Mas	no·s	tanh	qu'ieu	la·n
qu'un	bai –	sar	Li	po – gues	tol –	r'o	em –	blar;	E	si	pueys	s'en	i –
dom –	n'a –	mar.	No	m'en	cal	plus	as –	sai – ar;	Ais –	si	cum	li	plai –
las	ho –	nors,	Qu'a –	vi – a	tro –	bat	ail –	lors;	Ans	vol	que	sai	mi
la	do –	lors?	Si	vals	dels	pla –	zers	me –	nors	Mi	faitz	tant	que	joys
			Envoi 1. Chan	– so –	ne –	ta,	vai	de	cors	Dir	a	mi – dons	que·t
			Envoi 2. Dal	– fi,	so –	latz	et	a –	mors	E	cor –	tes	sens	vos

m'en	—	ten	—	da	E	que·l_____	belh	ni	—	en_____	n'a	—	ten	—	— da.
re	—	pren	—	da	Si	tot_____	s'es	vers	qu'ilh_____	me	—	spren	—	— da.
-rais	-si	—	a	Vo	—	lun	—	— tiers	lo	li_____	ren	—	dri	—	a.
-ra,	si	—	a,	Qu'ieu	l'a	—	ma	—	rai	to	—	ta	vi	—	a.
de	—	stren	—	ha	·Per	tal_____	que	no·m	vol_____	ni·m	den	—	— ha.
m'en	ven	—	ha,	Sol	qu'a_____	vos	non	de	—	sco	—	ven	—	— ha.
re	—	ten	—	ha,	Pus	mi_____	re	—	te	—	ner_____	non	den	—	— ha.
es	—	sen	—	ha	Cos	—	si_____	joys	e	pretz_____	vos	ven	—	— ha.

Milan, Biblioteca Ambrosiana, MS R 71, f. 49v; Paris, Bibliothèque National, MS fr. 20050, f. 88v.
S. C. Aston, *Peirol* (Cambridge, 1953), pp. 81–4.

This melody, which is much more simple in style than the three previous examples, is a vers, i.e. a melody which does not have any internal repetition.

TRANSLATION

To her who banished me from her side will I make reparation for the wrong she has herself committed, for I am yet minded to return to her, if it please her, my songs and myself without hope of any other favour; only may she permit me to seek her love and to await therefrom some trifling reward.

Never on account of any hurt that may come upon me do I cease to seek her friendship; on the contrary, I suffer the resulting grief and tribulation to consume me. She ought, indeed, to do me some favour, but it is not seemly that I should reproach her, although it is true that she behaves badly.

My thoughts dwell on her night and day and I know not how to help myself. But if it were possible, I would fain steal or snatch a kiss from her; and if she then grew angry thereat, right willingly would I restore it to her.

Well do I know that I could not turn my heart from loving her, either on account of anger or distress or to love another lady. I care not to strive against her further; as it please her, so let it be, for I will love her always.

There is no man in the whole world so completely subjugated by love for it does not even permit me to retain the pleasures or the marks of favour that I have found elsewhere; on the contrary, it would fain have me languish here for such a one who desires me not and scorns me. Fair lady, in whom good sense, worth, and beauty dwell, will you thus allow desire and grief to overwhelm me? At least, provided it befits you, grant me some of the lesser pleasures so that joy may come to me.

Go quickly, O song, and tell my lady to keep you since she does not deign to retain me in her service.

Dauphin, may pleasure, love and courtly good sense teach you how you may attain joy and worth.

18. L'autrier m'iere levaz

Pastourelle   Anonymous (later 12th century)

Paris, Bibliothèque National, MS fr. 20050, f. 91v.
K. Bartsch, *Altfranzösische Romanzen und Pastourellen* (Leipzig, 1870), pp. 121–2.

The *pastourelle* was a poetic genre dealing with love in a rural setting, very often describing the efforts of a passing knight to seduce an unwilling (or not-so-unwilling) peasant girl. This example has the musical form aab which is to be found in many trobador songs and in the great majority of trouvère songs. The two 'a' sections are not always exactly the same, while the 'b' section may be of any length and may sometimes quote from the 'a' material. The strong rhythm of the text and the syllabic melody suggested a metrical transcription. The text is hybrid, a sort of French imitation of Provençal.

TRANSLATION

The other day I had arisen and mounted my horse and then went riding for pleasure along a meadow. I had not gone far when I stopped and stepped down in the field under a flowering branch. There I saw Ermenjon. No flowering rose nor any crystal could match her. Happily and gaily I go towards her, for her beauty attracts me.

When I had drawn near, I said to her 'Sister, love me and you will receive honour throughout your life.' 'My lord, do not make fun of me. I know well that you will easily find a woman to love who is richer and better dressed than I.' 'Lovely one, I do not seek high birth in love. I take

pleasure in sense and beauty, of which you have much, and sweet companionship.'

'You are talking nonsense, for you will take nothing away with you from this place, for love is promised to somebody else. If you don't get back on your horse and go away quickly you are sure to be unlucky, because Perrin is watching us, and there will be lots of shepherds to help him if he calls out.' 'Lovely one, do not be afraid, but listen to me. Now *you* are talking nonsense.'

'Sir, at least I beg you to be merciful to me. If I stay here I shall surely come to harm.' 'Lovely one, I promise you, if you have me for your lover, no man will be bold enough to insult you. For God's sake, be my mistress.' 'Sir, do not say such things. Not even for all that I saw in Limoges on Tuesday would I grant your wish.'

'Shepherdess, this is how things are; I am a fool to carry on asking. There's no pleasure in harping on the same string.' I drew her to me; she gave a cry which nobody heard. She didn't struggle too much, but said gently to me 'Sir, I was upset when you arrived. Now my heart is gay; your caresses have restored my spirits.'

19. Chanterai por mon coraige

Chanson de Croisade (1189) with refrain   Guiot de Dijon (late 12th century)

R 21 ; Paris, Bibliothèque Nationale, MS fr. 846, f. 28r.

The work of the trobadors was known and admired far outside the borders of Provence, certainly as far away as northern France and

northern Italy and Spain. During the second half of the 12th century there arose in northern France a similar literary movement whose members, writing not in the langue d'oc but in the langue d'oïl – the forerunner of modern French – were known as *trouvères*. Like the trobadors, their ranks included both aristocrats and commoners. By about 1300 the trouvère movement itself had virtually disappeared, **extingu**ished partly by the beginning of a fashion for polyphonic chansons. The taste for monophonic song did not, however, wholly disappear; Machaut was still writing unaccompanied chansons in the mid-14th century.

Most of the genres of trobador poetry had their trouvère equivalents – *canso/chanson, alba/aube, sirventes/serventois, planh/plaint, tenso/tenson* or *jeu-parti, pastoral/pastourelle, chanson de croisade,* etc. A majority of trouvère songs have melodies in aab form, although the relative length of the a and b sections and the literalness of the repetition are extremely variable. Those poetico-musical structures which at the end of the 13th century came to be known as the *formes fixes* – the *ballade, rondeau,* and *virelai* – are not in fact often to be found in the trouvère repertory, being far more common in polyphonic than in monophonic songs. Trouvère melodies tend to be less elaborate than those of the trobadors, and they are often notated in a more rhythmically explicit manner. This enables more plausible rhythmic interpretations to be made, although as with the trobador pieces we do not claim that our transcriptions are definitively 'correct', only that – to us – they seem musically satisfactory.

In *Chanterai por mon coraige* a lady reflects on the absence of her lover, who is away on crusade. The melody blends exact and varied repetition, its apparent simplicity concealing a high degree of art. The 'Entrée' of our main source has been changed to 'Outrée' in conformity with other sources of this song.

TRANSLATION

I will sing to keep my courage up, since I must comfort my heart, for in my great distress I do not wish to die, or go mad, when I see anybody return from the savage land where he has gone who soothes my heart when I hear him mentioned.
God! when they shout 'Quick march!' O Lord, help the pilgrim for whose sake I tremble, for the Saracens are treacherous.
That is why I grieve in my heart, because he is not near at hand; I have placed my hopes in him, and now I get no pleasure or joy from it. Since he is handsome and I am nobly born, Dear Lord, why have you done this? Seeing that we are in love with each other, why do you keep us apart? *God* . . .

I shall be waiting in anguish until I see him come back. He has gone off as a pilgrim. In fear and trembling I will wait for him to come back, for in spite of my family I have no intention of marrying any other. He who suggests this is mad. *God* . . .

What grieves me is that I did not go with him. He sent me the shirt which he wore for me to hold in my arms. At night, when love of him torments me, I take it to bed and hold it to my naked body, to ease my suffering. *God* . . .

This solace at least I have seeing that I have accepted his pledge. When the gentle wind blows which comes from a most fair land, where the man I love so much is now, I turn my face towards it; I cannot resist fondling it [the shirt] under my grey blanket. *God* . . .

20. Gaite de la tor

Aube Anonymous (*c.*1200)

R 2015; Paris, Bibliothèque Nationale, MS fr. 20050, f. 83r–v.
K. Bartsch, *Chrestomathie de l'Ancien Français* (Leipzig, 10/1910),
pp. 166–7.

The melody of this aube or dawn-song is cast in the common aab form, and the 'a' sections are given *ouvert* and *clos* endings, corresponding to the modern 'first time' and 'second time' bars. A semi-dramatic performance of this song has been suggested by Alfred Jeanroy. The first five verses should be sung alternately by two singers representing watchmen conversing with each other, while verses six and seven should be sung by a third singer playing the part of the lover on whose behalf watch is being kept. The interjections 'hu et hu . . .' may indicate the playing of a horn or trumpet by one of the watchmen.

TRANSLATION

'Watchman on the tower, watch all round the walls, as if God were watching you, for the ladies and their lords are at rest, and robbers are on the prowl.' Hu and hu and hu and hu! 'I have seen one over there, deep in the hazel copse.' Hu and hu and hu and hu! 'I could almost have killed him.'

'Friend, I would sing you a pretty love-song about Blanchefleur were it not for my fear of the miscreant.' Hu and hu and hu and hu! 'I saw him over there, deep in the hazel copse.' Hu and hu and hu and hu! 'I could almost have killed him.'

'Friend, I am wrong, for I would willingly have slept in that tower. Don't be afraid! Let him pass unmolested whoever wishes to travel by this road.' Hu and hu and hu and hu! 'It must remain a secret, friend, this turn of events.' Hu and hu! 'I know well that we will gain much amusement from it.'

'They are not very numerous, these robbers: I can see only one, who lies "in clover" under the blanket, and I would not dare to name him.' Hu and hu and hu and hu! 'Let it remain a secret, friend, this turn of events.' Hu and hu! 'I know well that we will gain much amusement from it.'

'Courtly lover, resting at your ease in the peaceful chamber, do not be afraid, for you can sport until daytime.' Hu and hu and hu and hu! 'Let it remain a secret, friend, this turn of events.' Hu and hu! 'I know well that we will gain much amusement from it.'

'Watchman on the tower, watch for my departure from the spot where I heard you. From my sweetheart and our love-making in this tower I have realized that I was even more in love.' Hu and hu and hu and hu! 'I have lain so short a time in this love-nest.' Hu and hu! 'The dawn which makes war on me has annoyed me very much.'

'Saving God's honour, I could always wish that night could be made of the day. Then I would never experience grief or sorrow.' Hu and hu and hu and hu! 'I have surely seen the triumph-song of beauty.' Hu and hu! 'That goes without saying. Watchman, goodbye, all the same.'

21. La flours d'iver

Chanson   Guillaume le Vinier (*c*.1190–1245)

R 255; Paris, Bibliothèque Nationale, MS fr. 20050, f. 52r.
P. Mérard, *Les Poésies de Guillaume le Vinier* (Geneva, 1970), pp. 72–4.

Like the previous example, this melody is in aab form, with ouvert (bar 8) and clos (bar 16) endings for the 'a' section. Despite the gender, the 'Lord Nonesuch' in the *envoi* is probably a pseudonym for the poet's beloved.

TRANSLATION

It pleases me so much to gaze at the winter flower on the branch that Love reminds me anew to sing a song. I want to praise those beneath her spell, and hate and blame those who, though free from torment, bring themselves to complain about love.

Whoever wishes to deceive Love does himself a disservice. The whole world must spurn such villainous behaviour. Whoever could exact revenge for this ought to strive to right the wrong of deceit in love.

The one who conquers his lady-love through pretence works to his own great dishonour. He cannot deceive himself more. What joy, what pleasure is there in wasting the good things of love without savouring them? It is a great villainy, and greater shame.

For the ache and the pain double love's blessings, for whomsoever wins them through suffering and by enduring torment. Since one must place one's trust in loving truthfully, I ought to endeavour to win it earnestly, without deceiving. It is in such happy expectation that I myself can seek my joy. For never could pretence or trouble find their places there. They go and frequent the hypocrites! I want to renounce them: they want to extinguish all honourable behaviour.

Little song, I cherish you so much that I make Lord Nonesuch listen to you. In him true worth can dwell and remain.

22. Au renouvel du tens

Pastourelle in lai form   Anonymous (13th century)

R 980; Paris, Bibliothèque de l'Arsenal, MS 5198, ff. 340-1.

The *lai* was the secular equivalent of the *sequence,* employing each melodic phrase twice for successive lines of the lyric. In a *strophic lai* each stanza of text is set to the same music. *Au renouvel du tens* incorporates a refinement of the basic lai form in restating the second melodic unit at the end, producing the musical form aabbccbb. The 'b' section has ouvert and clos endings.

TRANSLATION

At the renewing of the season, when the little dark blue and white flower is coming out in the fields, I saw beneath a hazel-tree, picking violets, a lady as pretty as a fairy, and her companion. She was lamenting to her friend about two admirers whom she had, and whose sweetheart she was. One is poor, but courtly, gallant, more generous than a king, and handsome without blemish; the rich one has vast possessions, it is true, but in him there is neither good looks, nor feeling, nor courtesy.

'Take my advice, gentle sister. Love the rich one; you will profit greatly by it. For if you desire money, you will have plenty of it from him, and never lack anything that he has. It is good to love the rich man, for he has plenty to give. I would be his sweetheart. If I forsook

a scarlet cloak for one of coarse wool I would be acting foolishly. The rich man wishes to love and have a good time, while the poor man wishes to enjoy you without giving his sweetheart anything.'

'Now I have heard your advice, fair sister: I would not love the rich one for anything. Truly, he will never be my lover, for that means breaking my heart; A lady who has a noble heart would do no such thing. Ladies who wish to love with affection and without pretence should never expect any reward – whatever anyone may say and however much we may be slandered – except sweet true love. I hate all women who make love with men for what they get out of them, and may Jesus Christ curse them, for that is sheer licentiousness.

'Oh, true Love, you have so utterly forgotten me that night and day I can scarcely bear it. His remarkable handsomeness has greatly disfigured and made pale my beauty. I think of him so much by night and by day that I am altered in every way. Nightingale, go and tell him of the anguish which I suffer for him, and yet I do not complain at all – tell him that he will have my love, for he will never get anyone more beautiful or better than me – tell him that he will have plenty [of love] once I am his sweetheart, and that he need not hesitate to take full pleasure from life.'

23. Il covient qu'en la chandoile

Chanson capcaud in vers form   Perrin d'Agincourt (*c.*1220–*c.*1300)

R 591; Paris, Bibliothèque Nationale, MS fr. 846, f. 66r–v.

In a *chanson capcaud* the first line of a stanza ends with the same rhyme as that which ended the last line of the previous stanza. The melody of this example is through-composed.

TRANSLATION

A candle must be threefold in substance before it is worth anything or has the power to do its duty. For it must indeed have wax and a wick, and the top must be lighted, and then it is ready to serve others until it is burned and melted away.

Thus is my case and condition, alight with the fire cast by love which makes my heart burn and pains my body, melting it away without hope of cure. This fire came from above. I felt it strike me when I had seen that before which a mountain peak prostrates itself, from which I burn, sigh, and desire.

My heart is downcast in despair, and ekes out a poor existence, for, to tell the truth, the heart which falls into despair through long waiting for a reward seems a false champion when it has grown well and happy again. But I have chosen to die in the dominion of Love, who burns and kindles me.

24. Cuidoient li losengier

Chanson in rotrouenge form   **Guillebert de Berneville (13th century)**

R 1287; Paris, Bibliothèque de l'Arsenal, MS 5198, p. 145.

There is a disagreement concerning the precise meaning of the term *rotrouenge*. It seems to indicate a type of simple refrain structure with the refrain occurring as the last line of each stanza. This example is composed in the familiar aab form. 'Losengiers' or scandal-mongers were a recognized object of abuse in the trobador-trouvère repertory.

TRANSLATION

The scandal-mongers thought that because they have lied I must keep my distance from Love and my sweetheart. In God's name, I will love him, and serve true love night and day, without falsehood, and will enjoy myself, singing and merry.

I do not seek to flee from the slanderers. Yes, I will say, I will love my dear sweetheart. Dear God, if only he were here now! He is so handsome, so fair, so true at heart that I have never seen anyone more gallant. I know love, and there is nothing better in the world, and I take my pleasure from it, singing and merry.

In my heart I have a messenger of courtly and honest love who restores me to happiness, for every day he speaks to me. He has told me that I will overcome the slanderers and prove them wrong. They will rue the day, the liars, and I will enjoy myself, singing and merry.

Slanderers, false gossipers, I don't give an ear of corn for you! Now may your schemes collapse! I have a heart so fearless that I will embrace my sweetheart as soon as I see him. At this you will be downcast and I will amuse myself, singing and merry.

Little song, you will go to my sweetheart, whom I have accepted, and say to him that, by God, he should not forget the body of which he has seized the heart. He must never give up because of the slanderers; I know them to be wicked and cowardly. Die now, slanderers, cry for mercy, and I will enjoy myself, singing and merry.

25. Dex est ausi comme li pellicans

Sirventois in vers form   **Thibaut de Navarre (1201–53)**

R 273; Paris, Bibliothèque Nationale, MS fr. 846, ff. 37r–v.
H. van der Werf, *The Chansons of the Troubadours and Trouvères* (Utrecht, 1972), pp. 124–5.

This moralizing poem by one of the most famous of the trouvères is set to a vers or non-repeating melody which exists in several different versions. The product of a largely oral culture, trobador and trouvère melodies were naturally liable to alteration, and where concordant versions of a melody exist they are rarely the same in all respects.

In verse 4 Thibaut alludes to 'the book of the Britons' – i.e. Geoffrey of Monmouth's *Historia Regum Britanniae*, completed in about 1136. The 'castle' is Vortigern's tower, which collapsed every time it was rebuilt because under it there slept two dragons – a red dragon symbolizing the British people, and a white dragon symbolizing the Saxons who were to defeat them.

TRANSLATION

God is like the pelican, which builds its nest in the tallest tree. And the evil bird which comes from below kills its baby pelicans, because it is so foul. The worried and distressed father comes back and kills itself with its beak, and immediately makes its little ones revive with its grievous blood. God did the same thing at the time of His passion: with his sweet blood He redeemed His children from the Devil, who was so powerful.

The recompense of this is small and slow in coming, for there is no longer any good or justice or pity: instead pride and deception take first place, and felony, treason, and presumption. Our condition is now one of very great peril. But for the example of those who are so fond of

quarrels and battles – that is to say the churchmen who have abandoned their sermons to make war and kill people – nobody would believe in God any more.

Our head gives us pain in all our limbs, and it is just that we complain of this to God. And the barons are also greatly at fault, since it grieves them when somebody wishes to do a good deed. In their relations with other folk they do much that is to be condemned, as ones who know so well how to lie and cheat. They make this evil-doing return to them, for whoever seeks evil should not fail to receive it. If a man is striving with all his might to combat a small wrong, a great wrong should not remain in his own heart.

We should read, in the story which is to be found in the Book of the Britons, the battle of the two dragons, which caused the castles to fall down. It is his world which must tumble, if God does not put an end to the battle. Merlin had to make his prophecies to make clear what was going to happen. But you may know that the Antichrist is coming, in the clubs which the Devil controls.

Do you know who are the vile, stinking birds, who are killing God and his children? It is the *Papelards* [i.e. religious hypocrites] whose name is so filthy. By their falsehoods, these foul, stinking, vile, and evil people kill off all the simple folk who are the children of God.
Papelards make the world rock [on its foundations]. By St Peter, it is a bad thing to meet them. They have taken away joy and solace and peace. They will carry this great burden in hell.

Now may God let us serve and love Him, and the Lady who must not be forgotten, and may He keep us forever from the evil birds, who have poison in their beaks!

26. Dame, merci

Jeu-parti   Thibaut de Navarre (1201–53)

1. Da - me, mer - ci, u - ne rien vos de - mant. Di - tes me
2. Par Deu, Thie - baut, se - lonc mon e - sci - ant A - mors n'iert
3. Da - me, cer - tes ne de - vez pas cui - dier, Mais bien sa -
4. Thie - baut, tai - siez, nus ne doit co - men - cier Rai - son qui
5. Da - me, Dex doint que vos ju - giez a droit, Et co - nois -

voir, se Dex vos be - ne - ï - e, Quant vos mor - rez et je,
ja por nu - le mort pe - ri - e, Ne je ne sai se vos
- voir que trop vos ai a - me - e. De la joi - e m'en aing
soit de touz droiz des - se - vre - e. Vos le di - tes por moi
- siez les max qui me font plain - dre, Que bien sai, quelx que li

mais c'iert a - vant, Car a - prés vos ne vi - vroi - e je mi - e,
m'a - lez gui - lant, Que trop mai - gres n'e - stes en - co - re mi - e.
plus et toing - chier, Et por ce ai ma grais - se re - co - vre - e,
a - mo - loi - er, En - con - tre vos que tant a - vez gui - le - e.
ju - ge - menz soit, Se je en muir A - mours co - vient a fain - dre

Que de - van - ra A - mors, ce - le es - ba - hi - e, Qui tant a - vez sens, va -
Quant nous mor - rons (Dex nos doint bo - ne - vi - e) · Bien croi qu'A - mors do - ma -
Qu'ainz Dex ne fist si tres be - le riens ne - e Con vos, ma Dame, mout me
Je ne di pas, cer - tes, que je vos he - e, Mais se d'A - mors me co -
Envoi. Se vos, Da - me, ne la fai - tes re - main - dre De - danz son leu ar - riers
Thie - baut, s'A - mors vos fait por moi de - strain - dre Ne vos griet pas, que, se

- lour, et j'ain - tant Que je croi bien qu'a - prés nos iert fail - li - e.
- ge j av - ra grant Mais touz jors iert va - lors d'A - mors com - pli - e.
fait es - mai - er Quant nos mor - rons qu'A - mors se - ra fi - ne - e.
- ve - noit ju - gier, E - le se - roit ser - vi - e et ho - no - re - e.
ou e - le e - stoit, Qu'a vo - stre sen ne por - roit nuns a - tein - dre.
a - mer n'e - stoit J'ai bien un cuer qui ne se sau - roit fain - dre.

R 335; Paris, Bibliothèque Nationale, MS fr. 846, f. 37r.

The *jeu-parti* was a favourite form among the trobadors and trouvères. It consisted of an imaginary debate, usually between the poet and his lady-love or between one poet and another, on an aspect of the theme of courtly love. The melody of *Dame, merci* takes the familiar aab form.

TRANSLATION

Lady, have mercy, I ask a favour of you. Tell me truly – God bless you – when you die, and I – but that will be first, for I could not live after you – what will become of Love, that fool; for you have so much wisdom and worth, and I love so much, that well do I believe that after us Love will perish.

In God's name, Thibaut, in my opinion never will Love perish because of anyone's death, and I do not know if you are deceiving me, for you are not too thin at present. When we die (God grant us a good life) I well believe that Love will suffer greatly, but Love's true worth will always live on.

Lady, in truth you must not think so, but realize that I have loved you greatly. The joy this gives me makes me love and esteem myself the more, and because of this I have regained my sleek appearance, for never did God make born as lovely a creature as you, but it gives me great dismay that, when we die, Love will come to an end.

Thibaut, be quiet: no one should embark upon a discourse devoid of common sense. You are saying this to soften me towards you, me whom you have deceived so much. I do not say, in truth, that I hate you, but if I had to pass judgement on Love, she would be well served and honoured.

Lady, God grant that you judge rightly, and recognize the ills that cause my complaining, for I know well that whatever the judgement, if I die as a result, Love must become a matter of pretence, unless you, lady, make her stay in the place where she was, for none can attain your wisdom.

Thibaut, if Love causes you distress for my sake, let it not grieve you, for, even if it was embittered, I have a heart which could not deceive.

76

27. Lo'ntellecto divino

Lauda   Anonymous (Italian, early 14th century)

(Liuzzi)

MS.   Ripresa

Lo'n - tel - le - cto di - - vi - no de l'al - to lu - -

- me con gran - de splen - do - re, rag - gio de - gno d'o - no - re, a Sie - n'à da - to'l

no - vel A - gu - sti - no.   De no - bel - tà et gen - til na - ti - o - ne, a la re -

- li - gi - o - ne mi - ra - cu - lo - sa - men - te fu do - na - to; cum san - cti - tà et re -

- cta'n - ten - ti - o - ne fu - gi pre - la - ti - o - ne, d'ap - pe - ti - to d'o - nor sem - pre spo - lia - to.

Chi è l'al - bor guar - da - to nel pa - ra - di - so da

quel che - ru - bi - no, se no'l nuo - v'A - gu - sti - no ch'eb - be nel mon - do sin - gu - la - re sta - to?

Florence, Biblioteca Magliabechiano, MS. Mus. II I 122, f. 122.
Fernando Liuzzi, *La lauda e i primordi della melodia italiana* (Rome, 1935),
II, p. 361.

(1) MS. BGACBCBABGAB for GEFABAGFGEFG
(2) and (4) MS. F clef for C clef   (3) MS. C for B

The *lauda* was a hymn of praise or devotion sung by the many penitential fraternities in Italy during the 13th and 14th centuries. The monophonic melodies seem to be mainly secular in origin, and in some cases the original text of a non-religious song is known to have been replaced by a more spiritual text. Many laude are written in *ballata* form (see No. 74) – an opening refrain or *ripresa,* two lines or units of lines sung to new music and called *piedi,* a line or unit of lines sung to the refrain music and called a *volta,* and a repetition of the text and music of the refrain: the form A (refrain) bba (stanza) A (refrain) resulted, and there were usually several stanzas. In this example the text of only the refrain and first stanza is printed. We give the music in two versions – our own unmeasured transcription, which does not impose a rhythmic interpretation on the non-rhythmic notation, and Liuzzi's mensural reconstruction. The fact that two such divergent treatments are possible emphasizes the very equivocal nature of much pre-ars nova notation.

TRANSLATION

The new Augustine has given to Siena divine understanding of the heavenly light with great splendour, a ray worthy of honour. He who was of noble and gracious parentage was miraculously given to the religious life; with rectitude and holiness he shunned preferment, always free from ambition for honour. Who is the morning light, watched in paradise by that cherub, if it not the new Augustine, who had a unique position in the world?

28. Nas mentes senpre tẽer

Cantigas de Santa Maria   Anonymous (Spanish, late 13th century)

Esta é como Santa Maria fez parecer nas pedras omagẽes a ssa semellança.

The refrain is sung after every verse.

El Escorial, MS j.b.2, 29; MS T.j.1, 29; Madrid, Biblioteca Nacional, MS 10069, 29.
W. Mettmann (editor), *Alfonso X, O Sabio, Cantigas de Santa Maria* (1959), I, pp. 88–9.

The music of the trobadors and trouvères was known and admired in Spain and Portugal during the 13th century. A comparable repertory of Spanish origin quickly grew up, but practically all Spanish secular lyrics survive without music. There remain, however, over 400 sacred songs or *cantigas,* the majority of which are addressed to the Virgin Mary or recount miracles attributed to her. Alfonso X 'The Wise', King of Castile (1230–84), had these *cantigas de Santa Maria* copied into sumptuously executed manuscripts, three or four of which survive, and he is said to have written some of the poems himself. Many of the cantigas describe miracles of the Virgin to simple, mainly syllabic melodies which make considerable use of internal repetition, as in this example. The dialect of most of these cantigas is Galician-Portuguese, even when the composers are Castilian. Similarly, Catalan trobadors continued to compose in Provençal until the second half of the 13th century.

TRANSLATION

This song tells how the Blessed Virgin caused images in her own likeness to appear in stone.

We should always carry in our minds the features of the Virgin because they were imprinted upon hard stones.

According to what I've heard from men who have been there, in the Garden of Gethsemane were found likenesses of the Mother of God, and they were not paintings.

We should always . . .

Nor indeed were they carved, God forgive me, and there was there the face of our Lady of Graces holding her Son, and [her features were] properly made according to her measure.

We should always . . .

Thus, she made them appear and glow so brightly, so that we must believe that she is Lady of the natural order and has the power to make dark things clear.

We should always . . .

God chose to fashion them in stone in order to show us how the whole of creation should honour His Mother, because He came down from on high to take flesh in her.

We should always . . .

29. Maldito seja quen non loará

Cantigas de Santa Maria in villancico form   Anonymous (Spanish, late 13th century)

Esta é de loor de Santa Maria.

El Escorial, MS j.b.2, 290.
W. Mettmann (editor), *Alfonso X, O Sabio, Cantigas de Santa Maria*
(1959), III, pp. 97–8.

Every tenth song in the *Cantigas de Santa Maria* is entitled 'in praise of
Saint Mary' and has a devotional rather than a narrative text. This
example is written in *villancico* form, the Spanish equivalent of the French
virelai and the Italian ballata – *abbaabbaa* etc. The villancico structure in
fact underlies a majority of the songs in the *Cantigas,* sometimes being
present in slightly varied forms. It may also be traced in the previous
example.

TRANSLATION
This song is in praise of the Virgin Mary.
Cursed be the man who will not praise her who embodies all virtues.

Cursed be he who will not praise her who had no peer in virtue, nor
shall have as long as the world endures: for God did not, and shall not,
create another like her.
Cursed be the man . . .

Blessed forever be the man who praises so noble and honoured a Lady
to whom God was born, man and Saviour: he will be rewarded for it
hereafter.
Blessed be the man who will praise her who embodies all virtues.

Cursed be he who does not extol her in whom none of the attributes of
goodness or worth is wanting, and who never will lack any of them.
Cursed be the man . . .

Blessed be he who always serves the Mother of God, Virgin without
blemish, because when he departs from this world she will bring him to
the presence of her Son.
Blessed be the man . . .

Cursed be he who will not speak fair of the best of good women,
refusing to receive her love while he can: for through it he will win the
love of God.
Cursed be the man . . .

Blessed be he who rejoices in praising such a Lady who made us have
the love of God, acknowledging her who will intercede for us all.
Blessed be the man . . .

30. Polorum regina

Pilgrim song: ballo rodò   Anonymous (Spanish, 14th century)

sce - le - ra. | 1. An - te par-tum vir - go De - o gra - vi - da, | Sem - per per-man-
2. Et in par-tu vir - go De - o fe - cun - da, | Sem - per per-man-
3. Et post par-tum vir - go ma-ter e - nix - a. | Sem - per per-man-

– si - sti in - vi - o - la - - - ta. Stel - la ma-tu - - ti - na, de - le sce - le - ra.
– si - sti in - vi - o - la - - - ta. Stel - la ma-tu - - ti - na, de - le sce - le - ra.
– si - sti in - vi - o - la - - - ta. Stel - la ma-tu - - ti - na, de - le sce - le - ra.

7 MS. G for F

E–*MO*, f. 4r.

This strophic composition from the *Llibre Vermell* of the monastery of Montserrat in Spain is a pilgrim song and is called a *ballo rodò* presumably because of the repeated return of the second half of the melody with the refrain text. The music must have enjoyed considerable popularity because it was printed by Francesco de Salinas in his treatise *De musica liber septem* (Salamanca, 1577) with a villancico text *Yo me iba, mi madre*.

TRANSLATION

REFRAIN: O queen of all the heavens, O morning star, efface our sins.
1: Before the birth, O virgin pregnant with God, you were always pure. O morning star, efface our sins.
2: And in childbirth, O virgin, you were fruitful with God. O morning star, efface our sins.
3: And after the birth, O virgin, you were a dutiful mother. O morning star, efface our sins.

31. Under der linden

Minnelied   Walther von der Vogelweide (*c.*1170–*c.*1230)

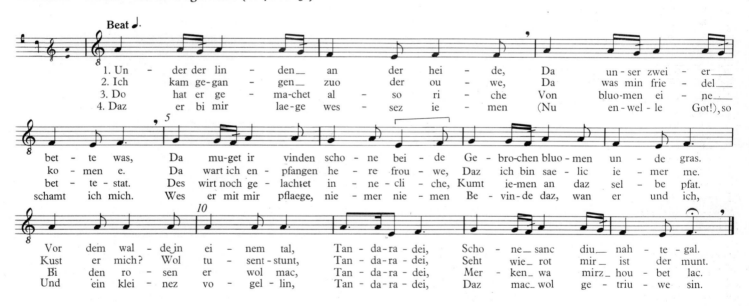

Beat ♩.

1. Un - der der lin - den__ an der hei - de, Da un - ser zwei - er__
2. Ich kam ge-gan - gen__ zuo der ou - we, Da was min frie - del__
3. Do hat er ge - ma-chet al - so ri - che Von bluo-men ei - ne,__
4. Daz er bi mir lae-ge wes - sez ie - men (Nu en-wel - le Got!), so

bet - te was, Da mu-get ir vinden scho - ne bei - de Ge - bro-chen bluo - men un - de gras.
ko - men e. Da wart ich en - pfangen he - re frou - we, Daz ich bin sae - lic ie - mer me.
bet - te - stat. Des wirt noch ge - lachtet in - ne - cli - che, Kumt ie-men an daz sel - be pfat.
schamt ich mich. Wes er mit mir pflaege, nie - mer nie - men Be - vin-de daz, wan er und ich,

Vor dem wal - de_in ei - nem tal, Tan - da-ra-dei, Scho - ne_sanc diu__ nah - te - gal.
Kust er mich? Wol tu - sent-stunt, Tan - da-ra-dei, Seht wie_ rot mir_ ist der munt.
Bi den ro - sen er wol mac, Tan - da-ra-dei, Mer - ken_ wa mirz_ hou - bet lac.
Und ein klei - nez vo - gel - lin, Tan - da-ra-dei, Daz mac_ wol ge - triu - we sin.

Paris, Bibliothèque de L'Arsenal, MS 5198, p. 366.
O. Sayce, *Poets of the Minnesang* (Oxford, 1967), pp. 103–4.

The flowering of German secular song between the 12th and 14th centuries came about partly through the growth of a native poetic tradition and partly through assimilation of Provençal and northern French culture. German songs of this period are known as *Minnelieder* (*minne* = *amour courtois,* or courtly love) and their creators are called *Minnesinger*. Actually two main types of poem and song existed – the *Minnelied* proper, or courtly love-song, and the *Spruchdichtung,* which was a more serious type roughly equivalent to the sirventes. Like trobador songs, Minnelieder seldom survive in rhythmically explicit notation. The metre of the German language makes modal rhythmic interpretation less universally appropriate to the minnelied repertory than it is in trouvère chansons, duple metre or free rhythm sometimes being preferable. Some lieder, especially the earlier ones, are *contrafacta* of troubadour or trouvère songs, a German poem replacing the original

lyric. *Under der linden* uses the melody of an anonymous trouvère chanson *En Mai au douz ten nouvel*, the German text fitting the first-mode rhythm of the poem whose place it takes. Like Neidhart, Walther came from the Austro-Bavarian area.

TRANSLATION

Under the linden on the heath, where we made our bed, there you may find prettily plucked flowers and grass. Before the wood in a valley, tandaradei, sweetly sang the nightingale.

I walked to the meadow where my lover had already come. I was greeted as a high-born lady, for which I shall always be joyful. Did he kiss me? At least a thousand times, tandaradei; see how red my mouth is.

There he made a bed, rich with flowers. Whoever passes along that pass would laugh. He can see by the roses, tandaradei, where my head lay.

If anybody knew (God forbid it!) that he lay with me, I would be shamed. What happened there may no one ever know except he and I and a small bird, tandaradei, which can be faithful.

32. Owê dirre sumerzît

Minnelied in Bar form   Neidhart von Reuenthal (*c.*1190–*c.*1240)

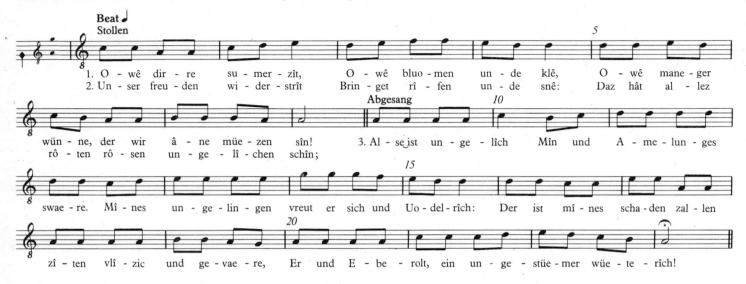

Berlin, Preuss. Staatsbibl., Cod. germ. 779, f. 240.
E. Wiessner, *Die Lieder Neidharts* (Tübingen, 1963), p. 89.

Like many minnelieder, this example is in what is known as *Bar form*, consisting of two poetic units called *Stollen*, sung to the same melody, and a concluding unit called an *Abgesang*. The music for the Abgesang may repeat part or all of the Stollen melody or, as in this song, its melodic material may be entirely new. The basic aab structure of Bar form is to be found also in many trobador and trouvère songs. Neidhart's home may have been in Bavaria, but the 'Riuwental' to which he refers has not been positively identified with any modern placename; later he was patronized

by the Austrian Duke Frederick II and seems to have lived near Vienna. He specialized in poems with a winter or summer setting. The melody of this song is preserved in an apparently corrupt version which we have treated rather freely.

TRANSLATION

Alas, the dear summertime; alas, the flowers and the clover; alas, the many joys which we must forego! Frost and snow now oppose our happiness: everything has a look quite unlike the red roses of summer; thus is my sorrow unlike that of Amelung. He and Uodelrich rejoice at my misfortune. He is always busy plotting to injure me, he and Eberolt, an uncouth brute.

33. Ez ist hiute eyn wunnychlicher tac

Spruchdichtung in Bar form   The Tannhauser (*c.*1200–1266)

(1) First time. (2) Second time.

-mey - ne. Also ich der ma - ge müz un - per,— Daz ich dort vriun - de vyn - de,— Die
my - ner kunf - te wer - den vro,— Daz ich ge-hey- zen müge eyn sel - den - ri - chez in - ge - syn - de.

Jena, Universitätsbibliothek, MS, f. 42v.

Internal melodic repetition is evident in the Abgesang of this expressive piece, and the Abgesang closes with a phrase from the end of the Stollen. Whatever information we have about the Tannhäuser is gleaned from personal references in his works. These paint a picture of an adventurous life which included participation in the crusade of 1228–9 and in the Cyprian war which took place two years later. The death of the German Emperor Frederick II removed one of the Tannhäuser's main sources of patronage, and the last years of his life were spent wandering from court to court supporting himself meagrely with his songs. He died in 1266.

TRANSLATION

Today is a joyful day. Now may He who has power over all things keep me in His care, so that I may be blessed and atone for my great guilt. For He can certainly help me to save my soul, and be free from sin and still win the grace of God.

Now let Him give me such a steadfast spirit that I may earn God's thanks, so that my end will be good and my soul happy, my departing sweet. May purity help me to be spared from hell, and grant me what I desire, that I may share in the highest joy. When I have to leave my kinsmen, may I find friends there who will rejoice at my coming, so that I may be accounted one of a blessed company. (There follow sixty more lines.)

34. Myn vroud ist gar czugangyn

Spruchdichtung in Bar form   Heinrich von Meissen ('Frauenlob') (d.1318)

Stollen

Myn vroud ist__ gar czu-gan-gyn,_ Nu ho - rit ia-mir-li - che__ clag, Mich rü - wit my-

-ne sün - de Di ich be - gan - gyn__ han myn ta-ge; Der ist__ ley-dir al - so__ vil Nu wil

der tot_____ mich breng der werld czu__ nich - te.—Myn le-byn wert nicht lan - ge,— Der tot myn en - de

hot ge - sworn, Waz ich an yn ge-sen-de Das__ ist_____ al - lis_____ gar vor-lorn,— Wen he mich__

Abgesang

myt__ ym ne-myn__ wil,_____ O - we der ia - - -mir-li - chin czu vor-sich - te.__ Mich

hilft nicht vrey__ ge - mu-te,_____ Noch kun-de-keyt,_ noch o - byr - müt,__ Noch al-lir_____ vrou-wyn

gu - te._____ Myn tognt,_ myn kraft,_ myn syn-nyn,_____ Das ist al - lis gar vor-lorn;__ Der mich czu ge-sel-

-lin_ hot dyr_____ korn_ Das ist der tot_____ myt dem mus ich von__ hyn - nyn.__

Vienna, Nationalbibliothek, MS 2701, f. 17r.

In this Spruchdichtung the two Stollen are not exactly the same, and the last line of the Stollen reappears at the end of the Abgesang.

Also known as 'Frauenlob', Heinrich von Meissen belonged to the last generation of Minnesinger. Born in about 1260, he came from central Germany. He travelled widely as a singer and in about 1312 went to

Mainz in the service of Archbishop Peter von Aspelt. He died there in 1318.

TRANSLATION

My joy has completely vanished; now hear a wretched lament. I repent of my sins that I have committed in my time; there are, alas, so many of them. Now death will destroy my life in this world. My life will not last long; death has sworn my end. Whatever petitions I make to him are all wasted, for he wants to take me with him. Alas for this lamentable certainty. Cheerfulness does not help me, nor does knowledge or pride or the kindness of ladies. My virtues, my strength, my senses – these are all completely lost. The one who has chosen me is death, and with him I must depart from here.

35. Ich warne dich

Spruchdichtung in Bar form   **Wizlaw** (*d.*1325)

Jena, Universitätsbibliothek, MS, f. 77r.

A few Minnelieder, including this example, are extremely florid in style and would seem to have been intended for a virtuoso singer. The moralizing tone of the poem is typical of the Spruchdichtung genre. Internal melodic repetition will be observed in the Abgesang. Wizlaw came from northern Germany.

TRANSLATION

I warn you, young man, tread gently, be charitable in outlook. Be mindful of the good that will follow your doing good. Shun bad advice. All the saints will receive you and your pure soul in God's high kingdom.

36. La quinte estampie real

Estampie   **Anonymous (French, 13th century)**

Paris, Bibliothèque Nationale, MS fr. 844, f. 104v.

The *estampie* was an instrumental dance whose musical form was similar to that of the vocal lai. It consisted of a number of sections or *puncti*, each of which was repeated (sometimes with different ouvert and clos endings). In this example each punctus has the same pair of endings.

The Ars Antiqua

37. *Examples of Organum from* Musica Enchiriadis

37a Strict simple organum at the fifth

Vox Principalis

Tu Pa – tris sem – pi – ter – nus es Fi – li – us.

Vox Organalis

37b Strict composite organum at the fourth

V.O.

V.P. Tu Pa – tris sem – pi – ter – nus es Fi – li – us.
V.O.

V.P.

37c Strict composite organum at the fifth

V.O.

V.P.
V.O.

Sit glo – ri – a Do – mi – ni in sae – cu – la, lae – ta – bi – tur Do – mi – nus in o – pe – ri – bus su – is.

V.P.

37d Free organum

V.P.

V.O. Rex cae – li, Do – mi – ne ma – ris un – di – so – ni,
Ti – ta – nis ni – ti – di squa – li – di – que so – li.

37e Free organum

V.P.

V.O. Te hu – mi – les fa – mu – li, mo – du – lis ve – ne – ran – do pi – is,
Se ju – be – as fla – gi – tant, va – ri – is li – be – ra – rē ma – lis.

M. Gerbert, *Scriptores Ecclesiastici de Musica* . . . (St Blaise, 1784), I, pp. 164, 166, 167, 169 and 170.

The musical illustrations in the 9th-century Frankish treatises *Musica Enchiriadis* and *Scholia Enchiriadis* are the earliest known examples of *polyphony* – i.e. of music in which two or more melodic lines are sounded at once. This primitive polyphony, which was known as *Organum,* came into existence in the same area as and only a little later than the practices of troping and sequence composition, and like them its purpose was to adorn and elaborate the liturgy. It did so by adding another vocal line – the *vox organalis* – to an existing plainchant – the *vox principalis.* In early organum the added part lay underneath the plainsong. The two voices proceeded in exactly parallel motion a fifth or fourth apart (37a: strict simple organum). To enhance the sonority the plainsong could be doubled an octave lower and/or the vox organalis could be doubled an octave higher (37b and c: strict composite organum). Of greater importance for the future was the technique of free organum, which, in order to avoid the harmonic tritone which certain melodic progressions in parallel motion would produce, abandoned parallelism in favour of more independent part-movement. The usual procedure was for the voices to begin on a unison, for the vox organalis to remain on the initial pitch until the plainsong had moved a fourth or fifth away from it, and for the two voices then to move in parallel intervals until the end of the phrase, when they returned to a unison in a variety of ways (37d and e: free organum).

TRANSLATION

Thou art the everlasting Son of the Father. (From the *Te Deum.*)

May the glory of the Lord endure for ever; the Lord shall rejoice in his works. (From Psalm 103 (104).)

King of Heaven, Lord of the roaring sea, of the shining sun and the dark earth, Thy humble servants, by worshipping with pious phrases, beg Thee to free them – at Thy command – from their sundry ills.
(Although given as separate examples, 37d and e set words from the same Sequence.)

38. *Alleluia* Te martyrum

Free organum   Anonymous (School of Winchester, *c.*1050)

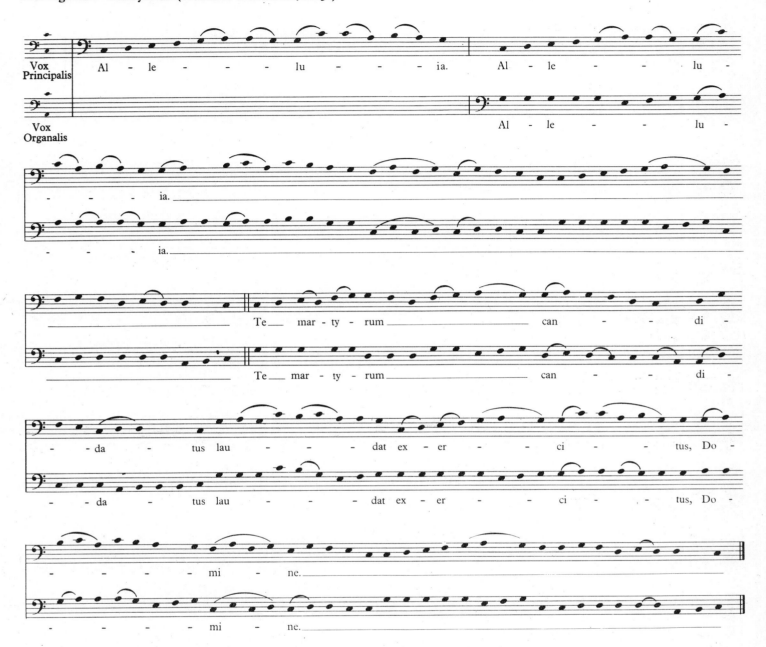

The Alleluia section was repeated.
Cb 473 55 A. Holschneider, *Die Organa von Winchester* (Hildesheim, 1968) pp. 163–4.

After *Musica Enchiriadis* there are few surviving examples of organum until the early 11th century. One source – particularly important in that it preserves a large working repertory rather than a few brief examples illustrating a treatise – is the Winchester Troper of *c.*1050. For many years the notation of the manuscript was considered indecipherable, but recent research suggests otherwise. The Winchester organa – settings of Kyrie and Gloria tropes, Alleluias, Sequences, etc. – bear out the information on organum given by Guido of Arezzo in his treatise *Micrologus* of about 1025. Free organum is the preferred type, with parallel, contrary, similar, and oblique motion being intermingled and with the voices occasionally crossing. The vox principalis continues to be the higher of the two parts, which move almost entirely in note-against-note fashion. The existence of the Troper shows that polyphonic composition had spread from France to England by the early 11th century.

TRANSLATION

Alleluia. The noble army of martyrs praise Thee, O Lord. Alleluia.

39. *Alleluia* Justus ut palma

Free organum   Anonymous treatise *Ad Organum Faciendum* (*c.*1100)

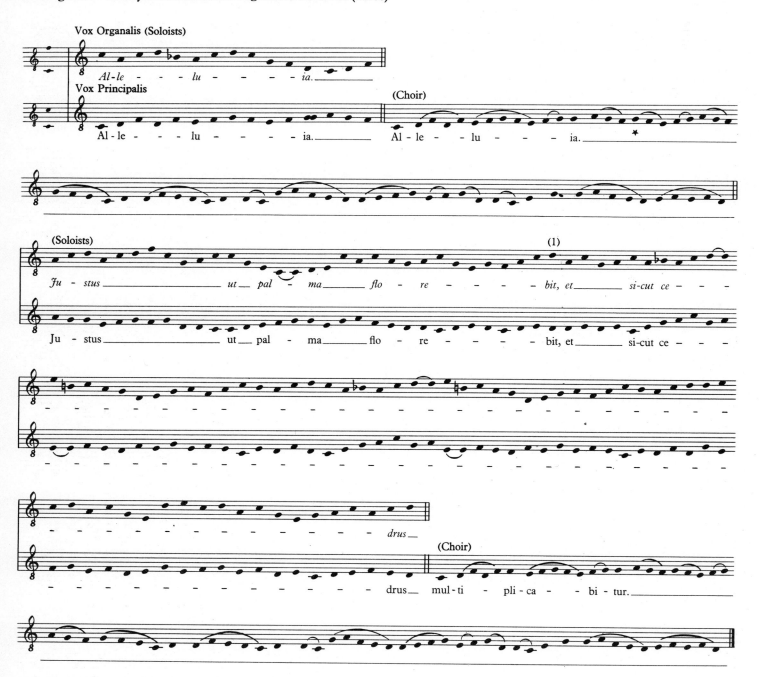

(1) Vox Organalis: D not in MS.

The polyphonic Alleluia was repeated and was followed by the plainsong Alleluia from the asterisk to the end.
Berlin, Staatsbibliothek der Stiftung Preussischer Kulturbesitz, MS theol. lat. qu. 261, f. 48v; Milan, Biblioteca Ambrosiana, MS 17 Supp., f. 58r.

Dating from about 1100, the anonymous French treatise 'On the Composing of Organa' is the earliest source to place the vox organalis above the vox principalis, thus creating what came to be the standard relationship between a plainsong and a newly-composed voice. In this example from the treatise only those portions which would be sung by soloists are provided with an organal part. This practice, which was possibly suggested by the difficulty which a choir might have experienced in reading and learning melodies outside the usual plainsong repertory and in singing them against a more familiar melodic line, also remained standard for the rest of the medieval period.

TRANSLATION
Alleluia. The righteous shall flourish like a palm-tree, and shall spread abroad like a cedar in Libanus. Alleluia.

40. Rex omnia tenens

Troped *Benedicamus Domino*   Anonymous (School of St Martial, *c.*1150)

St M–D 11.

This and the next example are taken from one of the so-called 'St Martial manuscripts'. These sources preserve a repertory emanating from Southern France between about 1100 and 1170, although they cannot be proved to have originated at the Benedictine Abbey of St Martial at Limoges. For much of the late 11th and 12th centuries this was culturally one of the most active parts of Europe, a major centre of trope, sequence, and polyphonic composition and the birthplace of the Trobador culture. An important stylistic innovation in the St Martial polyphony occurred through the introduction of passages in which the organal voice sang several notes over a single note of the *vox principalis*. The term *organum* came to be applied to this type of melismatic motion over a sustained plainsong note, while the hitherto prevailing note-against-note style became known as *discant*. In this troped *Benedicamus Domino* (the original words occur at the end of the text) the two styles have not yet become fully distinct. Polyphonic settings of *Benedicamus Domino* are common, and probably replaced a plainsong setting at the end of Matins, Lauds, or Vespers.

TRANSLATION

The King who holds sway over all things came from His mother's womb like a bridegroom bright from the marriage chamber, like the sun at dawn sending its light in rays everywhere. Thus the prophet foretold in his words 'A light is risen among the people'. With a joyful heart, let us therefore bless the Lord.

41. De monte lapis

Anonymous (School of St Martial, *c.*1150)

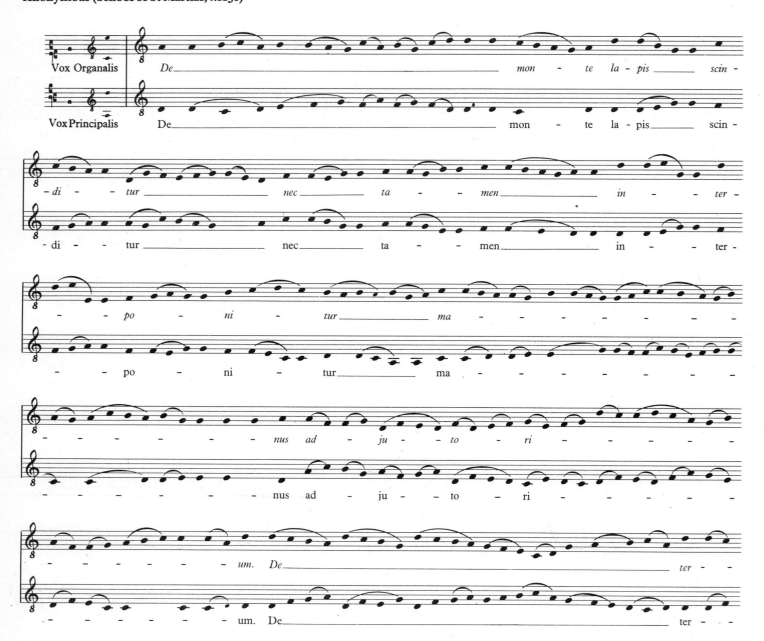

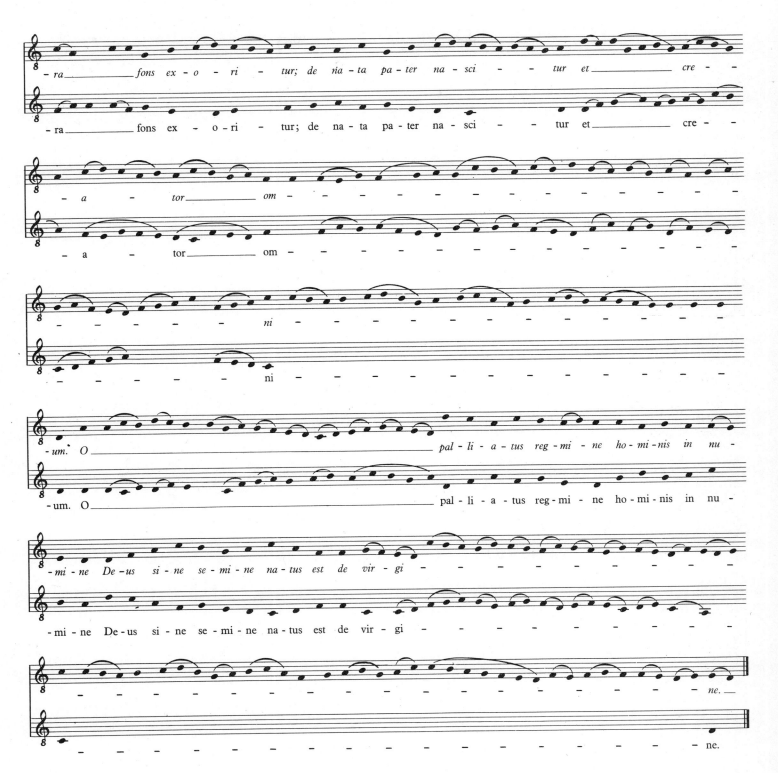

St M–D 24.

This example shows a clearer and more self-conscious differentiation between the organal and discant styles, the latter being used for the main body of the text while the former is reserved for the cadential points. The text is not liturgical and its function is uncertain.

TRANSLATION

A stone is broken off from the mountain but no helping hand is introduced. A fountain springs from the earth; the father and creator of all things is born from his mother. Protected by the hand of a man according to the divine will, God is born of a virgin without human seed.

42. *Kyrie* Rex immense, Pater

Troped Kyrie (Codex Calixtinus, mid–12th century)

Vox Organalis

Vox Principalis

1. Rex im - men - - se, Pa - ter pi - - e, e - - - lei - son. 4. Chri-ste,
2. So - ther, the - - os a - tha - na - - tos, e - - - lei - son. 5. Qui de
3. Pal - mo cun - - cta qui con - clu - - dis, e - - - lei - son. 6. Tu - um

Fi - li Pa - tris sum - mi, e - lei - son. 7. Con-so - la - tor dul - cis a - mor, e - lei - son.
cae - lis de - scen - di - sti, e - lei - son. 8. Qui Ja - co - bum il - lu - stra - - sti, e - lei - son.
pla - sma re - de - mi - sti, e - lei - son. 9. Cu - jus pre - ce no - bis par - ce, e - lei - son.

Compostela 16.

Although the manuscript known as the 'Codex Calixtinus' has been in the possession of the Monastery of Santiago at Compostela since the 12th century, it shows evidence of French influence. Its twenty–one polyphonic pieces are similar in style to the St Martial compositions. The text of this troped Kyrie is a mixture of Latin and Greek.

TRANSLATION

Great King, dear Father, have mercy. God, immortal Saviour, have mercy. You who hold everything in Your hand, have mercy. O Christ, great Son of the Father, have mercy. Who came down from heaven, have mercy. You who redeemed Your own blood, have mercy. Comforter, sweet Love, have mercy. You who made James famous, have mercy. By [James's] prayer spare us; have mercy.

43. *Alleluia* Non vos relinquam *with clausula-motet* Homo quo vigeas/Homo quo vigeas/Et gaudebit

Organum duplum and three-voice clausula-motet: Alleluia at Mass on Ascension Day.
Anonymous (Organum from period of Léonin, *c*.1170; clausula- motet from period of Pérotin *c*.1200)

Beat ♩.
(Soloists)

(Duplum)

Al - - - - -

(Tenor)

Al -

-le

-le

(Triplum) Ho - mo, quo vi - ge - as vi - de. De - i fi - de - i ad - hae - re - as,

(Duplum/Motetus) Ho - mo, quo vi - ge - as vi - de. De - i fi - de - i ad - hae - re - as,

A¹ I   II etc.
et gau - de -

in spe gau - de - as et in fi - de in - tus ar - de - as fo - ris lu - ce - as.

in spe gau - de - as et in fi - de in - tus ar - de - as fo - ris lu - ce - as.

Tur - tu - ris re - tor - que - as os ad a - scel - las, do - cens i - ta ver - bo vi - ta

Tur - tu - ris re - tor - que - as os ad a - scel - las, do - cens i - ta ver - bo vi - ta

o - ris vo - me - re de cor - di - bus fi - de - li - um. E - vel - las lo - li - um, li - li -

o - ris vo - me - re de cor - di - bus fi - de - li - um. E - vel - las lo - li - um, li - li -

- um in - se - re ro - sae, ut a - li - um per hoc cor - ri - pe - re spe - ci - o - se

- um in - se - re ro - sae, ut a - li - um per hoc cor - ri - pe - re spe - ci - o - se

A²

208 Triplum: MS. G

Alleluia: F 128.

Clausula-motet: F 824.

There arose during the middle of the 12th century a school of polyphonic composition centred on the new cathedral of Notre Dame at Paris (begun in 1163). The achievements of this Parisian school were remarkable. Its first known master, Léonin (*fl. c.*1170), composed polyphonic settings of the solo portions of Responsories, Graduals, Alleluias, etc. for the major feasts of the church year, many of these settings being subsequently revised and brought up to date by his successor Pérotin (*c.*1160–*c.*1225). Léonin was famed chiefly as a composer in the organal style, writing melismata of great length and freedom over the sustained notes of the plainsong. At about this time the sustaining function of the vox principalis led to this voice being called the *tenor* (from the latin *tenere,* to hold), while the vox organalis became known as the *duplum* or second voice. We will use these terms from now on. Léonin also wrote in discant style. Organum and discant usually alternate in Notre Dame compositions, the former being preferred when the plainsong tenor has only one note to a syllable and the latter being preferred when the plainsong is melismatic. Pérotin introduced the technique of composition in more than two parts, sometimes adding a *triplum* and even a *quadruplum* above the tenor-duplum pairing. In modernizing Léonin's music he replaced some of the organal passages with sections in the then more popular discant style. Much of his output in fact consists of *clausulae* – short compositions in discant style which have as their tenor a melismatic extract from a plainsong – which could be inserted at the appropriate point in a plainsong or existing polyphonic work. Clausulae often have a strongly repetitive rhythmic character with the upper voices moving in ternary metre over a tenor constructed as a repeated rhythmic pattern or *ordo.* In about 1200 the practice arose of adding texts to the upper part(s) of clausulae – an extension of the idea of troping. When provided with its own text a clausula duplum was called a *motetus*; hence arose the important genre of the *motet* – a composition with one or more independently-texted upper voices over a plainsong tenor. The explicit notation of rhythm appears for the first time in manuscripts of the Notre Dame repertory. It was devised chiefly in order to set down music in organum triplum, and the extent of its application to music in organum duplum is debatable. Our transcription of the organal sections of this Alleluia is, therefore, offered with due reservations.

In its original form the Alleluia *Non vos relinquam* was an entirely two-part composition, probably by Léonin. To the two-part discant-style setting of the tenor melisma on 'et gaudebit' Pérotin or a contemporary added a third voice or triplum; at about the same time this clausula was converted into a motet by the provision of the text beginning 'Homo quo vigeas' in the duplum and triplum. Two features of this clausula-motet are of special interest: the tenor is constructed as a repeated two-bar rhythmic phrase or ordo, and – for purely musical reasons – the plainsong melisma is stated twice. The development of these two principles of organization was eventually to culminate in the technique of *isorhythm.*

TRANSLATION

Motetus and triplum: O man, see how you should flourish. You should be true to God, rejoice in hope, and burn inwardly and shine outwardly in faith. You should turn the head of the turtle-dove back to its wings, thereby teaching by word of mouth that life comes forth from the hearts of the faithful. Pluck out the weed to sow the lily by the rose, so that by this deed you may grow splendidly strong in virtue to grasp the garlic [i.e. the weed]. You should be mindful for the well-being of everybody. You should hate all wicked pleasures. Consider your actions, because if you do not you will be damned. Do your duty to behave on this earthly road and think on the prize of the heavenly kindgom. And thus your heart will rejoice for ever.

Tenor: Alleluia. I shall not abandon you as orphans: I go and come to you, and your heart will rejoice. Alleluia.

44. Hypocritae, pseudopontifices/Velut stellae firmamenti/Et gaudebit

Double motet   Anonymous (French, *c.*1210)

(1) MS. E   (2) MS. C

(3) MS. C

F 875, Ba 74, Ma 86.

This motet also began life as a two-part clausula, to which a triplum and upper-voice texts were added. The following list of the guises in which this piece appears gives some indication of the protean nature of early polyphony:

1. A two-part clausula.
2. A two-part motet, a text beginning 'Virgo virginum regina' being added to the duplum.
3. A two-part motet, a text beginning 'Memor tui creatoris' replacing the text in (2).
4. A two-part motet, a text beginning 'O quam sancta' replacing the text in (3).
5. A three-part clausula, a triplum being added to (1).
6. The present three-part motet, with the texts 'Hypocritae' and 'Velut' added to the triplum and motetus.
7. A three-part motet, texts beginning 'El mois d'Avril' and 'O quam sancta' (as in 4) replacing the texts in (6).
8. A three-part motet, with texts beginning 'El mois d'Avril' and 'Al cor ai'.

The version printed here is an early example of the *polytextual motet* and is remarkably advanced for its date (about 1210). A motet with different texts in the motetus and triplum is called a *double motet*. The contrast between the two texts is emphasized by the dissimilar melodic lines, the triplum moving considerably more rapidly than the duplum in a fashion more common in mid-century compositions. The structure of the tenor is exactly as in the previous example.

TRANSLATION

Triplum: The hypocrites, false prelates, hardened killers of the church, clink their goblets in their boozy orgies. They sow the seeds of profit with tears; on their thrones they bellow like thunder; as judges and avengers they dishonestly accuse innocent supplicants, but they are false who give judgement. They give orders from their seats; they gloat over their treasures and purses in separate lurking-places. They offer their bitter sting as honey; they tell lies and make up errors in books and hide away their faces. Practitioners of lust and crime, they debase the coinage; they bear down on the poor with their judgements, making mud bricks out of straw. They destroy the good old pathways. O miserable state of those in high place! So many spectral heads cast a shadow over their ashes. A pallor shows on the face of the sad decadent Sabbath, and the plainness of emaciation; dishonesty lurks in the soul. O truth, that lies hidden under a cloud! O goodness, let terror grip the hypocrites, lest deceitful wickedness and deceitful falsehood harm you. O love, you avoid the hidden paths; you teach us to know what is right, for that is where you dwell.

Motetus: The deeds of the prelates shine forth like the stars in the heavens. They are the basis of the holy edifice, the fount of virtues, the way of rectitude, a graceful ornament, clouds yielding honey, winds making fruitful the earth, and the vine of the fields, rooting out worm, thorns and weed, sowing the lily in the hearts of the faithful. They separate the pure grain from the chaff; they reject earthly things for those of heaven. They bring illumination with the key of knowledge; they avenge crimes; they free the condemned with the key of their power. They do not cast a net for rewards, or turn their eyes towards purses. They pick out the tracks of the gentle lamb and direct the flock to the sweet pastures of life and glory. Their lamps not empty, they lead us to the royal marriage. May their pious prayers lift up our hearts.

Tenor: And [your heart] shall rejoice.

45. Quant florist/Non orphanum *or* El mois de Mai/ Et gaudebit

a. Bilingual double motet   Anonymous (French, *c*.1225)

b. Double motet   Anonymous (French, *c*.1225)

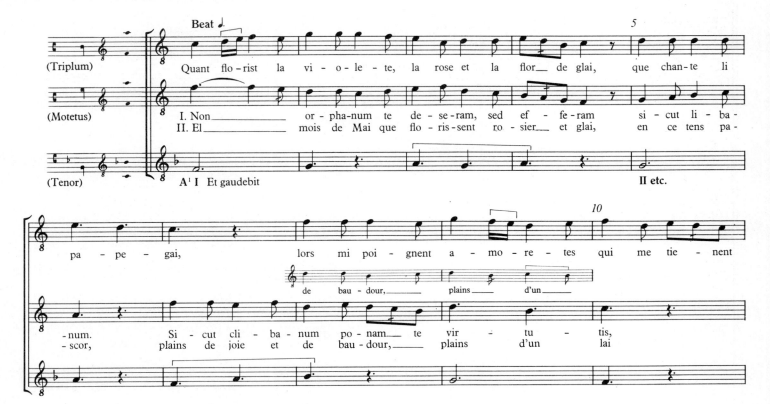

a. *Mo* 34, *Ba* 67.
b. *Mo* 126.

These two motets are derived from yet another clausula on the 'et gaudebit' melisma. The first is an example of the *bilingual motet,* a genre with a French triplum and a Latin motetus which had a fairly short currency during the 13th century. The second is a French double motet. Vernacular texts were being used in motet composition very soon after the genre came into existence; by the mid-13th century they preponderated over Latin texts, and the motet had become a courtly entertainment rather than an adornment of the liturgy. The tenor in this example has the same organization as in Nos. 43 and 44. The small notes indicate places where the *Non orphanum* motetus has been altered to fit the French text. 'Robechon' is a diminutive of 'Robin', a name often given to a shepherd-lad in a pastoral poem, as in Adam de la Halle's *Jeu de Robin et Marion.*

TRANSLATION

Triplum: When the violet flowers, and the rose and the iris, and when the parrot sings, then love affairs plague me, which keep me merry. But I have not sung for a long time. Now I will sing and make a pretty song for my sweetheart, to whom I dedicated myself a long time ago. God! I find her so sweet and true to me, and free from guile, that I shall never leave her. When I gaze at her mouth, her beautiful blonde head and her smooth throat, which is whiter than the lily flower in May, and her breasts so firm, pointed, and small, I wonder greatly where I discovered her. She is so wondrously fashioned that she rejoices all my heart. But I pray to the god of love, who spurs on lovers, that he will keep us in

honest love, true and perfect. May he curse those who watch us out of envy, for I will not desert her for wicked spies.

Motetus a: I shall not leave you orphaned, but shall lift you on high as frankincense. I shall place you there like a furnace of courage, like a drum and an organ of joy and safety. I shall lift off the yoke of Egyptian servitude. To my followers I shall bestow myself, as joy after tears, as a reward after the weariness of toil. When they have set out I shall come; I shall succour and bestow pardon through grace. I shall produce a pure and untroubled mind, the glory of those who dwell in heaven. I shall cast off the cares of the flesh and the burden of the world. The illustrious Holy Spirit will instruct your heart in divine matters and your spirit will utterly trust in the Lord, so that your coming in and your going out may be safe, and within you your heart will rejoice.

Motetus b: In the month of May, when the rose tree and the iris flower – at this Easter season, full of joy and gaiety, I sang a lai, riding, thinking, and playing a new love sonnet. I found a sweet, fair-haired, pretty young girl, all alone without a shepherd to guard her. She had a reed-pipe and a tabour; when it pleased her she sang and played a new love-song on the pipe. I stepped forward and greeted her with great courtesy and sat down beside her in the shade of a laburnum tree. With clasped hands I begged for her love. 'Pretty one, I will give you slippers embroidered with flowers, a skirt and a petticoat, a leather girdle, a brooch, a silken purse, a fine spring hat, if you will leave your shepherd-boy for me.' Crying 'Help! Help!' she answers 'I won't! I have no liking for false love. Never will I desert my Robechon for flower-embroidered slippers. On the contrary it is he whom I love and I shall continue to do so.'

Tenor: and [your heart] shall rejoice.

46. Cil s'entremet/Nus hom/Victimae paschali

French double motet   Anonymous (French, *c.*1250)

Mo 162, Ba 72.

G. Raynaud, *Recueil des Motets Français* (Paris, 1881), I, p. 156.

Of particular interest is the present example of a double motet with French texts. The tenor carries the well known Easter sequence, *Victimae Paschali laudes,* albeit only the first fifteen notes arranged in a rhythmical ostinato. In keeping with current practice the motetus and triplum frequently cross each other. In addition to its trochaic rhythm there are many instances of rhythmic motives in both voices such as the triplet figure and the descending four-note passage which act as unifying elements in the composition.

TRANSLATION

Triplum: He is foolish who wishes to speak against love, for honour and courteous behaviour are learned by loving, and for this reason one must not blame true love. He who wishes to find joy should cherish love faithfully and without deceit, and take care not to speak ill of his lady whom he must honour, for, if he speaks any evil of her, no comfort should he find.

Motetus: No one could know what it is to love with true love, for such a man suffers with hope that he might receive the sweet rewards, and serves loyally all his days who can have neither solace nor aid: it is fitting that he should receive nothing but evil and sorrow; from which it seems plain to me that it is great folly to love where one has no future, for it is travail without reward.

47. Psallat chorus/Eximie pater/Aptatur

Franconian motet   ? Franco of Cologne (*c*.1260)

Ba 30, Mo 51, Da 4, Hu 102, P11411 5, Westm 33327 8.

Thirteenth-century developments in musical style – in particular the

increasing independence between the voices of motets and the tendency to animate the triplum and motetus by breaking up and ornamenting their longs and breves – demanded a more versatile and precise method of expressing rhythm than the hitherto satisfactory *modal rhythmic notation*. The treatise *Ars Cantus Mensurabilis,* written by Franco of Cologne in about 1260, is a summary and codification of contemporary experiments in notation. Franco cites this motet to illustrate some of his remarks. The tenor is organized as a repeating two-bar ordo and, as in the previous examples, its melody is stated twice. Musically the work is conservative, and its use of Latin texts may indicate a non-Parisian origin.

TRANSLATION

Triplum: Let the choir sing a new song with tuneful melody in Thy name, O great Father. Protect us under Your shield, O Lord. O Nicholas, by your prayers place us with the angelic host and brotherhood of saints, which is prepared for us.

Duplum: O excellent and regal father, O pious ruler, O outstanding teacher, pray today to Jesus, the Son of Mary, on behalf of the servants of this church. O Nicholas, teach us today the true way of the heavenly kingdom, that we may enjoy the eternal rest which is prepared for us.

Tenor: . . . is prepared . . .

48. Excelsus in numine/Benedictus Dominus/*Tenor*

Double motet using voice exchange   Anonymous (English, late 13th century)

ONC 6.

This example illustrates the technique of *voice exchange* or *stimmtausch*. Except at the beginning and end and in the middle of the piece, the triplum and motetus exchange their melodies at regular four-bar intervals, producing this structure:

Triplum		A B C D		E F G H ;
Motetus	Introduction	B̂ A D C	middle	F E H G ending
(Bars)	7	4 4 4 4	3	4 4 4 4

Although voice exchange was common in Notre-Dame organa, its use in motets seems to have been an English peculiarity. It disappeared during the 14th century, though traces remained (see No. 64). The texts are in honour of St Thomas of Canterbury (martyred 1170).

TRANSLATION

Triplum: Raised up by the majesty of Your power, the Newly-born One has illumined us, His elect, with the light of his countenance; and in the person of Archbishop Thomas, his saint, He has led back into the true way one of our own number, exiled from His presence in error.

Motetus: Blessed be the Lord of the universe, who has illumined us with the gleam of his brightness; well disposed towards England, He has given us the aforesaid Saint Thomas as an advocate, and He has sanctified him.

49. Caligo terrae scinditur/Virgo Maria, filia/*Tenor*

Petronian motet   Anonymous (English, early 14th century)

(Triplum)
Ca - li - go ter-rae scin - di - tur, Per-cus - sa so-lis spi - cu - lo,

(Motetus)
Vir - go Ma - ri - a, fi - li - a re - gis al -

Tenor

Dum sol ex stel-la na-sci - tur, In fi - de - i di - lu - cu - lo;

- tis - si - mi, maes - tis sit re - me - di - a.

Re - bus-que jam co-lor re-dit Par - tu ni-ten - tis si-de-ris, Qua - rum de - co-rem pol-lu - it Pec -

La - te - ra con - sci - en - ti - a fa - ci - le sic il -

- ca - tum A-dae ve - te - ris. In par - tu pu - rae vir-gi - nis Nox ni-tet in-star lu - mi - nis;

- la - bi - tur ad fri - vo - la la - ben - ti - a.

Nox af-flu - it de - li - ci - is Pa - la-tis cae - li gau-di - bus. Per vi-sce - ra vir -

Quo la - que a - ta ra - pi - tur a - ni - ma sic il -

-gi-ne-a Fit val-lis fle-tus mel-le-a. Lau-dan-tes ca-nunt vi-gi-les; Gau-de-re
-lu-di-tur a fa-mu-la pro-pri-a si-ne

ju-bent fle-bi-les; In som-nes lu-strat cla-ri-tas; Lu-ctan-tes do-cet ve-ri-tas.
pro-vi-den-di-a. In te, vir-go, dif-fun-di-tur om-

San-ctae Ma-ri-ae gre-mi-um Vas est ho-rum ma-gna-li-um.
-nis po-ten-ti-a; haec au-di su-spi-ri-a.

ONC 9.

The subdivision of the breve, given formal recognition by Franco, was taken further by the theorist and composer Petrus de Cruce (*fl.*1290–1300). In the tripla of his motets Petrus divides the breve into as many as seven semibreves, exploiting to an extreme degree the current fashion for making the triplum the most lively voice in the texture. This example of the *Petronian* style comes from an important though fragmentary English source of the early 14th century. The greater incidence of small-note values in the triplum has led us to reduce the original note values by eight rather than by sixteen, and we adhere to this policy for numbers 50 and 56. *Caligo terrae* is by no means as eccentric in style as some Petronian compositions, whose tripla may contain so many syllables set to extremely short note values as to appear virtually unsingable. The tenor begins as a conventionally-repeating ordo but becomes irregular after two statements. The motetus was originally a French chanson *Mariounette douche,* whose *virelai* structure (abbaa) gives the motet its form.

TRANSLATION

Triplum: The darkness of the earth is broken, pierced by a shaft of light from the sun, while the sun is born of a star in the morning of faith; and now beauty returns to things on the bringing-forth of the star, for their beauty was spoilt by the sin of old Adam. By the labour of the immaculate Virgin night shines as bright as day; the night flows in joy with the delights of the heavenly palace. Through the Virgin's womb the valley becomes flowing with honey. The rejoicing watchmen sing; they order mourners to rejoice; brightness shines in the night; truth instructs the mourners. The lap of the blessed Mary is the vessel of these great events. *Motetus:* Let the Virgin Mary, daughter of the most high King, be a solace to those that grieve. Worthless thoughts easily degenerate into unworthy frivolities. There the enmeshed soul is captured and led astray from its own hand-maiden, without any good coming of it. In you, O Virgin, all power is poured forth; listen to our sighs.

50. O homo considera/O homo de pulvere/ *Contratenor*/Filiae Jerusalem

Isorhythmic motet   Anonymous (English, early 14th century)

ONC 17.

Although a few French motets of the 13th century have a quadruplum, motets for four voices did not become common until the 14th century. Several early examples occur in English sources, in which the fourth voice is often labelled 'quartus cantus'. It is usually textless and lies in the same register as the tenor. In the tenor part of the present example the concept of the repeated rhythmic cell or ordo is no longer evident; repetition is, however, apparent on a larger scale, the twenty-seven bar tenor melody being stated three times in the same rhythmic disposition. For a discussion of *isorhythm*, see No. 58.

TRANSLATION

Triplum: O man, consider what rewards the transient glory of the world gives, the nature of which encourages vain hopes. Now it flourishes; now it withers and the rewards which it brings are useless. Now it rejoices; now it weeps; peace, which would be pleasant to you, it brings and gives too late. I restrain these vices of my tongue as they struggle to follow Christ, and I seek to see the joy of heaven.

Motetus: O man, rise from the dust; quickly to embrace Jesus in heart, words, and deed, who for your sins was harshly killed and willingly underwent burial; He redeems you freely of His pure love. Therefore, wretch, rejoice in His path; shun all evil and strive to live so that you will be able to rejoice.

Tenor: O daughters of Jerusalem.

51. Pange melos lacrimosum

Conductus with cauda **Anonymous (French, c.1200)**

F775, W1 227.

The history and functions of the conductus are discussed in the commentary to the monophonic example (No. 13). *Pange melos* is typical of polyphonic conductus in that the text is given a syllabic treatment, the voices moving mainly in note-against-note fashion, i.e. in discant style. Like many conductus, this example ends with a melismatic passage called a *cauda*. The tenors of conductus are not based on plainsong. The last line of the second verse is missing from the manuscript and has been invented by the editors. The text probably laments the death of a monarch or eminent aristocrat.

TRANSLATION

O tearful elegy, sing a plaintive melody. A time of mourning has come, a time bereft of joy. At the eclipse the night of lamentation hides all things. Let grief prevail, because the reason for grief is plain to see.

The sinking star of the Rhine looks down on to Latin soil. The star falls. The star's fall enshrouds the earth in darkness. Truly the Latin region lies hidden, fearing to be seen. Night is the ally of mischief; [night is the parent of crimes].

52. Deus in adjutorium

Conductus   Anonymous (French, early 13th century)

1. De-us in ad-iu-to-ri-um   In-ten-de la-bo-ran-ti-um;
2. Ut cho-rus no-ster psal-le-re   Pos-sit, et lau-des di-ce-re
3. In te Chri-ste cre-den-ti-um   Mi-se-re-a-ris om-ni-um,
4. A-men, a-men, al-le-lu-ia,   A-men, a-men, al-le-lu-ia,

Ad do-lo-ris re-me-di-um   Fe-sti-na in au-xi-li-um.
Ti-bi, Chri-ste, rex glo-ri-ae: Glo-ri-a ti-bi, Do-mi-ne.
Qui es De-us in sae-cu-la   Sae-cu-lo-rum in glo-ri-a.
A-men, a-men, al-le-lu-ia,   A-men, a-men, al-le-lu-ia.

Mo 1, Ba 101, Da 1, Tu 3.

A conductus in three voices, without caudae.

TRANSLATION

O God, make haste to help those who are in travail; hurry to bring solace to those who sorrow. So that our choir may sing psalms and praises to Thee, O Christ, King of Glory: Glory be to Thee, O Lord. Have mercy on all those who believe in Thee, O Christ, who art God in glory for ever. Amen, amen, alleluia.

53. Praemii dilatio

Conductus with caudae   Anonymous (French, c.1210)

Prae-mi-i di-la-ti-o   me-ri-ti sup-
Prae-mi-i di-la-ti-o   me-ri-ti sup-
Prae-mi-i di-la-ti-o   me-ri-ti sup-

WI 171, *F* 632, *CbJ* 1 6.

A more elaborate conductus than the previous example, *Praemii dilatio* has a cauda after every line of text. Dissonances like that on the first beat of bar 13 are common in early polyphony; they result from the idea that in three- or four-part polyphony each upper voice had to be consonant with the tenor but did not need to be consonant with the other upper parts.

TRANSLATION

The postponement of a reward is a punishment for loyalty which, according to the proverb, results from the faults of great men, who delay recompense for the service of faithful men lest, the reward having been received, they should be less zealous in doing their duty. But the more a reward is postponed the more dearly is it sold. Bartered for long service, a gift loses its virtue.

54. Mundus vergens

Conductus   Anonymous (French, *c.*1210)

per ef - fe - ctum, se fal - la - cem___ ex - u - it. Nam re -
bel - li fa - ce, Gal - li - a___ prae - mo - ri - tur. Et jam

per ef - fe - ctum, se fal - la - cem___ ex - u - it. Nam re -
bel - li fa - ce, Gal - li - a___ prae - mo - ri - tur. Et jam

per ef - fe - ctum, se fal - la - cem___ ex - u - it. Nam re -
bel - li fa - ce, Gal - li - a___ prae - mo - ri - tur. Et jam

per ef - fe - ctum, se fal - la - cem___ ex - u - it. Nam re -
bel - li fa - ce, Gal - li - a___ prae - mo - ri - tur. Et jam

- mo - ta frau - dis ar - te nos de - le - re vi vel
na - vis ma - ri da - ta por - tu - ca - rens de - spe -

- mo - ta frau - dis ar - te nos de - le - re vi vel
na - vis ma - ri da - ta por - tu ca - rens de - spe -

- mo - ta frau - dis ar - te nos de - le - re vi vel
na - vis ma - ri da - ta por - tu ca - rens de - spe -

- mo - ta frau - dis ar - te nos de - le - re vi vel
na - vis ma - ri___ da - ta por - tu ca - rens de - spe -

ar - te quod jam pa - tet___ a - stru - it. Et dum hiis___ se ___
- ra - ta pro - ce - lis con - ci - ta - tur. Et fra - cta - (tur)___

ar - te quod jam___ pa - tet___ a - stru - it. Et dum hiis___ se
- ra - ta pro - ce - lis con - ci - ta - tur. Et fra - cta - (tur)

ar - te quod jam pa - tet a - stru - it. Et dum hiis___ se
- ra - ta pro - ce - lis con - ci - ta - tur. Et fra - cta - (tur)

ar - te quod jam pa - tet___ a - stru - it. Et dum hiis___ se
- ra - ta pro - cel - lis___ con - ci - ta - tur. Et fra - cta - (tur)

15—16 Triplum: a tone higher in MS.

ap — pli — cat,   quod ex — pli — cit _____ ex — pli — cat.
tur — bi — ne,   non e — get _____ re — gi — mi — ne.

ap — pli — cat,   quod ex — pli — cit _____ ex — pli — cat.
tur — bi — ne,   non e — get _____ re — gi — mi — ne.

ap — pli — cat,   quod ex — pli — cit _____ ex — pli — cat.
tur — bi — ne,   non e — get _____ re — gi — mi — ne.

ap — pli — cat,   quod ex — pli — cit _____ ex — pli — cat.
tur — bi — ne,   non e — get _____ re — gi — mi — ne.

F 5.

27 Triplum: E not in MS.

This is one of the few surviving conductus in four voices.

TRANSLATION

Declining into ruin, approving errors by its action, the world shows itself to be untrustworthy. For, as is patently obvious when the web of deceit is removed, it strives to destroy us by force or guile. And while it applies itself to these tasks it flaunts that which is transient.

Flowering for so long in peace, the world is now kindled by the torch of war, and France perishes before its time. And now the ship, consigned to the sea, cut off from port and given up for lost, is tossed by storms. And, battered by the hurricane, it does not lack guidance.

55. Beata viscera

Conductus-motet   Anonymous (English, late 13th century)

Be — a — ta vi — sce — ra Ma — ri — ae vir — gi — nis, quae

Be — a — ta vi — sce — ra Ma — ri — ae vir — gi — nis, quae

Be — a — ta vi — sce — ra Ma — ri — ae vir — gi — nis, quae

fru — ctu gra — vi — da ae — ter — ni ger — mi — nis in vi — tae po — cu —

fru — ctu gra — vi — da ae — ter — ni ger — mi — nis in vi — tae po — cu —

fru — ctu gra — vi — da ae — ter — ni ger — mi — nis in vi — tae po — cu —

Worc (91).

The text of this composition from the voluminous though badly damaged source known as the 'Worcester fragments' is a trope of the communion *Beata viscera*, whose plainsong is ornamented in the lowest part. The piece is something of a hybrid, motet-like in its plainsong basis and yet conductus-like in its score notation and note-against-note part writing. The presence of caudae at the beginning and end is another link with the true conductus repertory. The piece includes many chains of 6/3 chords which produce a typically English sonority and richness of texture. This

kind of parallel writing became a feature of the 14th-century English genre known as the *cantilena*, and it may have influenced the creation of the French technique of *fauxbourdon* (see No. 95) in the early 15th century.

TRANSLATION

Blessed be the womb of the Virgin Mary, which, pregnant with the fruit of the eternal seed, offers a drink of sweetness in the cup of life for us and for our sin.

'pro nobis et nostro vitio potum' is an editorial substitute for the illegible original text.

56. Hé, Diex! quant verrai

Polyphonic rondeau Adam de la Halle (*c*.1230–*c*.1288)

Ha 11.

Polyphonic settings of secular songs are rare before about 1300. The trouvère Adam de la Halle wrote several polyphonic chansons in a simple conductus-like style, most of which are in the form of the *rondeau*. During the later 13th century it had become fashionable to include refrains in the stanzas of secular lyrics. Three ways of doing this became so popular and stereotyped that they were called *formes fixes*, or set designs. Known as the *ballade*, *virelai*, and *rondeau*, they were to dominate the polyphonic song until the late 15th century. The *ballade* had

the musical form aab, like many trouvère chansons, with a textual refrain at the end of the b section. The *virelai* had the form AbbaA (capital letters indicate the textual refrain). The *rondeau* had a refrain at the end and in the middle of the stanza, producing the form ABaAabAB. *Hè, Diex!* exemplifies the *rondeau* design on a minute scale.

TRANSLATION

O God! when shall I see her whom I love? Truly, I don't know. O God! From looking at her pretty form I am dying of hunger. O God! when shall I see her whom I love?

57. Edi beo thu

Anonymous (English, later 13th century)

OCC 59.

Secular music in any form is extremely rare in England before the 15th century; like the present example, much of what does survive is religious or moral in tone. The frequent use of the third as a harmonic interval gives this piece a warmth and sonority which remained characteristic of English polyphony throughout the Middle Ages. The small notes are editorial suggestions for fitting the metrically irregular lines of stanzas 2 and 8 to the melody.

TRANSLATION

Blessed be you, queen of heaven, people's comfort and angels' bliss, spotless mother and pure maiden, such as no other in the world is. In you can easily be seen your precedence over all other women. My sweet lady, hear my plea and take pity on me if it be your will.

You rose up like day-break from the dark night. From you sprung a new sun-beam which has lit all the world. There is no maiden of your complexion, so fair, so pretty, so rosy, so bright. My sweet lady, take pity on me and have mercy on your knight.

When God wished to alight on earth, all for our sake, he wished no better than to take that maiden as his mate. He could not have done better, nor have taken a sweeter thing on earth. My lady, bring us to your bower and shield us from the terrors of hell.

The Ars Nova

58. Vos qui admiramini/Gratissima virginis/*Contratenor*/Gaude gloriosa

Isorhythmic motet   Philippe de Vitry (1291–1361)

58 Motetus: E for first D

94—6 Bottom stave two bars' rest only.

104 Bottom stave C for D.

I–IV 13, B–BA 758 4, F–CA 1328 47, GB–DRc 20 13.

Writing in about 1320, the French composer and theorist Philippe de Vitry produced a treatise on music which he entitled *Ars Nova*. Nowadays it is generally conceded that the extraordinarily rapid developments in music which occurred during the 14th century did indeed add up to a 'new art'. Polyphony flourished even in parts of Europe, such as Italy, where previously it had been hardly known. It became much more diverse, both in the number of techniques and styles which it encompassed and in the range of uses to which it was applied. Coherent construction on a very large scale became possible through the evolution of the *isorhythmic motet*. The secular song, hitherto almost always monophonic, was transformed into a predominantly polyphonic medium. Mensural notation attained maturity, achieving precision, versatility, and remarkable subtlety.

The *isorhythmic motet* was a logical development from those 13th-century motets in which the tenor melody had been organized as a repeated rhythmic *ordo* and had been stated more than once. The length of the rhythmic pattern gradually increased, so that instead of a two- or three-bar repeating ordo it came to be anything from about eight to about eighty bars in length, acquiring in the process the new name *talea*. The practice of restating the tenor melody continued, the melodic aspect of the tenor being called its *color*. While the upper voices of motets moved in the new short note values of the semibreve and the minim, the tenor often continued to move in longs and breves, consequently becoming a slowly-moving foundation of the polyphonic texture. Because of the length of the talea and the long duration of its individual notes the structural basis of an isorhythmic tenor could seldom be heard; this was considered not to matter since, merely by being present, its mathematical virtue informed the whole piece. In many isorhythmic motets the tenor is subjected to *proportional treatment* – i.e. the talea is restated in different note values, perhaps one half or one third those of the original statement, the mathematical relationship between the notes within the talea remaining the same.

This isorhythmic motet by de Vitry, which is mentioned by the 14th-century theorist Simon Tunstede, is typical of those being produced in the middle of the 14th century. Although it has six staves it is really in only four parts; the 'tenor solus' line was intended to replace the tenor-contratenor duo on occasions when only three-part performance was possible, and the 'tenor solus *Vivat iste*' line is a variant of it. The expansion of the motet texture from three parts to four came about during de Vitry's lifetime; as here, the fourth voice was usually a *contratenor* sharing the same range as and augmenting the supporting role of the tenor. The motetus and triplum frequently had different texts – a legacy of the 13th-century motet. In the tenor the long *Gaude gloriosa* melody is a *color* lasting 90 bars of the upper voices and arranged as six statements of a fifteen-bar *talea*; the *color* is then repeated as seven statements of a new nine-bar *talea*, with a partial eighth statement at the end. The contratenor has its own isorhythmic design. Although the upper voices are not completely isorhythmic, they contain sections in which rhythmic repetition does occur (compare the passages beginning at bars 100, 118, and 136). The effect noticeable in bars 100–3, in which a melodic line is broken up into isolated notes, is known as *hocket*.

TRANSLATION

Triplum: O you who admire maidens! If we are to be held more worthy than other men to marry the girl of our choice, when we have married her she must be greatly loved. This girl is beautiful in appearance, modest in mien, virtuous in deed: this other of yours is ugly, too aggressive in her boldness, and despising of good deeds. This one is the light, the cloudy night. This one is a swift eagle; you are the creeping snakes. This one reigns over you eternally languishing and wretched in a vale of misery. This sweet and royal maiden is my loving wife, who is faithful. I am a king, she my queen. What more shall we say? We who knew what we were doing have chosen a worthy wife, like a rose before the thorn. Hurry, therefore, to serve her, because time is slipping by and death pursues us. Summon her, because if you are negligent you will not see her, the glory which you desire. Make haste, then!

Motetus: 'O most pleasing image of a virgin, whom purity of body wholly adorns, deep down within me you have reconciled the innermost part of my heart with this sweet wound, kindling within me a spirit of love which knows no way out of my breast.' 'In the kindness of your heart you have employed all your womanly allures to inflict a similar wound on me. My queen, embrace your lover, and press my chest against your ample bosom.' 'O king of kings, join eye to eye and mouth to mouth in a kiss, and breathe a promise on your lips; and with this kiss let her become a goddess to her lover.'

Tenor: Rejoice, O glorious Virgin. (From the antiphon *Ave regina caelorum*.)

59. Alpha vibrans monumentum/Coetus venit heroicus/*Contratenor*/Amicum quaerit

Isorhythmic motet   **Anonymous (French, *c*.1390)**

59 Triplum: # for F after A

+ d2 × ½)

(2) 137 Motetus: G for A   (3) 141 Motetus: semibreve for breve

F–CH 564 105.

Some of the music written in France during the late 14th century attained a very high degree of stylistic, structural, or notational complexity, often associated with the setting of extravagantly-phrased, self-consciously 'literary' texts. Of the composers associated with this 'mannered school' – Solage, Trebor, Senleches, etc. – some had connections with the court of Gaston Phébus, Count of Foix (1331–91) or with the Papal court at Avignon. Although this isorhythmic motet is by no means as complicated as many of the 'mannered' compositions, the ingenuity with which its tenor is constructed is typical of the 'mannered school'. Its general style reveals the influence of Machaut in the use of duple metre, the frequent syncopations and the quickly-resolving ornamental clashes between the voices. The tenor consists of two statements of a long (70-bar) talea whose construction is described in a verbal canon. The color is divided into four phrases – A, B, C and D – of which A and B are used in talea I and C and D in talea II. Each phrase appears thrice – forwards, in retrograde in halved note values, and finally forwards in halved note values – and then the next phrase is manipulated in exactly the same way. The upper voices are also isorhythmic, bars 75–141 being a repetition of bars 5–71. Hocket appears in bars 33–36 and elsewhere. Our transcription moves freely between two-beat and three-beat bars.

The texts comment on the aims and beliefs of the Franciscans, frequently employing extravagant imagery drawn from various parts of the Bible, particularly from Revelation.

TRANSLATION

Triplum: When the Godhead shattered the statue, the auspicious jewel [Christ] was borne to fruition [Daniel 2]. The 'bright and morning star' becomes a portent of Egypt, soon brought forth into light. The onyx sparkling on the mountainside – a gem deep within – has now been lifted out, nowhere damaged, like a girl who is still virgin. The agate of revelation is discovered in the rock. So too the Prophet is discovered in the bed of the happy mother. The thyme spreads its green leaves, but it bears a snow-white splendour, like the Virgin Mother modestly holding the flower of the two of them. The new birth provides a new progeny, which offers itself as a sun to the earth's mass and the vast spaces of the universe. The stem and the flower bring forth a fruit which openly prophesies. The bridesman [St Francis] and his companions give equal praise on the sistrum and in a hymn. From the mountain tops the glorious citizens approach. The heirs of the magnanimous one come, singing loudly in praise. The watchful companions of the Most High say 'O humble people, come hither to the joy of the innermost heart.'

Motetus: Having imitated the life of the Son, the heroic throng approaches, whose seraphic prince [St Francis] was wonderfully transformed. Monks and nobility freely follow him, wearing his habit and leaving their paternal homes. Another holy man [?St Antony of Padua] enters and, like a man of Jerusalem, bows to St Francis who is borne on high like Elisha. St Francis proclaims 'I desire your property and fervently wish to have your companionship.' Garlanded with flowers [virtues], the other joyfully cries 'I rejoice, bound in your bonds and assured of poverty.' And he laid aside his flowers [money]. He chose flowers [virtues] through the new virgin birth and the conception of the heel (Genesis 3, 15). The swan and the dove come; the rose of the world, the joyful soul, the drummer of Francis (Exodus 15, 20), the pure virgin becomes joyful. Love of divine things and the prayers of musicians produced a holy, innocent character through the zeal of eager men.

Tenor: He seeks a former friend, who covered his nakedness with a garment in a monastery.

60. Gemma florens militiae/Haec est dies/
Contratenor/Tenor

Isorhythmic motet   Anonymous (Cypriot-French, *c.*1400)

10 Motetus: MS has semibreve

95 Motetus: C for D

I–*Tn 9 25.*

Cyprus had been ruled by the French family of Lusignan since 1192 and the culture of the Cypriot court was naturally francophile. The source of this isorhythmic motet is of Cypriot provenance and contains motets, chansons, and a very early example of the *tenor mass* (see note 85). The Janus mentioned in the motetus text was king of Cyprus from 1398 to 1432. The composition is isorhythmic in all voices, the triplum, motetus, and contratenor repeating exactly from bar 65 to the end. The tenor consists of two different colores; each color consists of a talea and its repetition in reduced note values. The source of the tenor melody is unknown.

TRANSLATION

Triplum: O glittering gem of courage, O gleaming badge of justice, may the people of Paris celebrate the mighty deeds and high praises of Macarius with little songs of joy, Macarius, through whose agency, together with France, Greece has celebrated, through the family of his distinguished progeny, the funeral rites of an impious race. He will not fear the punishments of idolatry, which come so quickly. With the cult of true religion he fortifies his sheep – worship which recommends moderation to people who lack faith. This shepherd of innocence explains for thousands the living message, in which message the prophets are so outstanding. The gods of the Gentiles reject their sacrifices of evil. May the compassion of the Godhead of Heaven, gleaming with the laurel-crown of glory, now reassure the King of Jerusalem, Armenia, and Cyprus, and those who rejoice with him today in the land of Thessaly, granting them promises of Heaven. Amen.

Motetus: This is the glorious day on which the noble Elizabeth brought forth her fruit, silencing taunts. She fulfilled the letter of the law, revealing the mystery. She is adorned with graces, strengthened with holiness before confinement. The herald was not yet born, yet truly he foretold a king, prophesying an empire. May he who washed all in the river Jordan preserve king Janus from the gloomy mist of error which hides the true light.

61. *Kyrie from* Mass of Tournai

Movement from polyphonic setting of Ordinary   Anonymous (French, earlier 14th century)

Sing sections I and II thrice each, section III twice and section IV once.
Bar 6 Motetus A for second C
Bar 8 Motetus E for F
Bar 10 Triplum FE for GF

B–Tc 476 I

Although individual mass movements had sometimes been set in polyphony during the Ars Antiqua period, it was not until the 14th century that polyphonic settings of all the items of the Ordinary (Kyrie, Gloria, Credo, Sanctus, and Agnus Dei) appeared. The Mass of Tournai is probably the earliest complete cycle to have survived. Dating from the first half of the century, it was probably assembled by a music copyist rather than being the work of a single composer. The Kyrie, Credo, Sanctus, and Agnus Dei are written in conductus style, while the Gloria uses the more independent rhythmic style characteristic of the Ars Nova.

TRANSLATION

Lord, have mercy. (Thrice)
Christ, have mercy. (Thrice)
Lord, have mercy. (Thrice)

62. *Agnus Dei from* Mass of Barcelona

Movement from polyphonic setting of Ordinary   Anonymous (French, mid-14th century)

53 Tenor MS. F for E.

E–*Bcen 971 5*– L. Schrade, *Polyphonic Music of the Fourteenth Century* (Monaco, 1956–68), I.

Another anonymous cycle of polyphonic settings of the Kyrie, Gloria, Credo, Sanctus, and Agnus Dei, the Mass of Barcelona (so called because of the location of the manuscript which preserves it) is rather more advanced in style than the Mass of Tournai. The tenor of the Agnus Dei has not been identified, although it resembles the portion beginning at 'qui tollis peccata mundi' of the Agnus Dei melody in the *LU* Mass XII. The movement is highly unified through brief snatches of imitation, by the five-bar sequence first stated in the triplum at bar 2, and by the hocketing passage beginning at bar 49.

TRANSLATION

For a translation, see No. 11q.

63. Gloria

Polyphonic mass movement   Gratiosus de Padua (Italian, late 14th century)

48, 65, 67, 69: all voices have Long.

I–Pu 684 7.

When Italian ars nova composers set items from the Ordinary of the Mass they usually did so in a style similar to that which they employed for setting secular texts. This idiom, which is sometimes called 'ballata style', is demonstrated in the present Gloria, in which a supple and ornate vocal line is supported by a tenor-contratenor duo. The tenor is, as usual,

freely composed. Of particular interest is the sequential pattern in the Amen section. Nothing is known of this composer except that he must have been active in Padua and that he composed both sacred and secular music. This Gloria may have been intended to form a pair with another surviving mass movement (a Sanctus) by Gratiosus.

TRANSLATION

For a translation, see No. 11c.

64. Sanctus

Mass movement in English descant style   Anonymous (English, _c._1370)

(The Hosanna was repeated.)

Taunton, Somerset County Record Office, MS D/D WHb. 3182, flyleaf.

In the written form of the originally improvisatory technique known as *English descant* a plainsong was 'harmonized' usually as the middle voice of three. The top voice or *descant* and the bottom voice or *counter* moved mainly in contrary motion against each other, and all three voices proceeded largely in note-against-note fashion. In this example the descant and to a lesser extent the counter are given some moderate ornamentation, particularly at cadence points.

TRANSLATION

For a translation, see No. 11n.

65. Gloria

Isorhythmic mass movement   ? Pennard (English, *c.*1390)

Je — su Chri — ste. Cum San — cto Spi — ri — tu, in glo — ri — a De — i Pa — tris.

82 Superius II: second D is semibreve

125 Superius I: second G is semibreve

GB–*Lbm 40011B* 1.

Although isorhythm had been employed in some French mass movements of the 14th century, the composition of fully isorhythmic mass movements became something of an English speciality. There are several examples in the late 14th-century source known as the 'Fountains fragment', from which this *Gloria* has been transcribed, and further instances occur in the 'Old Hall' manuscript (London, British Library, MS Add. 57590). The attribution of this work to the unknown composer Pennard rests on the stylistic similarity between the music and that of a Credo setting known to be by him, and also on the fact that the plainsong cantus firmi of both of these mass movements were taken from

Trinity Sunday. The Gloria tenor, not designated in the source, is the verse *Tibi laus, tibi gloria* of the Trinity antiphon *O beata et benedicta* (AS, pl. 293). The tenor color is stated four times, each statement containing four taleae; in the third and fourth statements the note values are halved. The contratenor has the same isorhythmic structure. The textless portions of the upper voices are also isorhythmic, but the texted parts are freely composed. The way in which these two voices 'duet' is very unusual; it is just possible that it has connections with the earlier technique of voice exchange.

TRANSLATION

For a translation, see No. 11c.

150

66. Credo

Mass movement in 'mannered' style   Lionel Power (*c.*1370–1445)

⌐⌐ = red notes; ⌐⌐ = void notes in O mensuration; ▽◁ = void notes in C mensuration.

GB–OH, 83.

This composition is taken from the Old Hall manuscript, the largest surviving source of English church music of the late Ars Nova period. The manuscript, which according to Dr Roger Bowers may have been copied for the household chapel of Thomas, Duke of Clarence and brother of King Henry V, contains a repertory of music for the Mass composed between about 1370 and 1420. The most frequently represented composer is Lionel Power, Master of the choristers in Clarence's chapel. Power's surviving music, which probably dates from between about 1390 and 1435, shows an astonishingly full stylistic development, from the simple descant pieces such as No. 67 through complex 'mannered' pieces like the present example, to the fully-developed cyclic mass *Alma redemptoris mater* of about 1425.

The rhythmic and notational complexity of this Credo suggest the influence of the 'mannerist' composers of France and Italy. Black notes, red notes, and void notes have to be interpreted differently in each of the three mensurations C, O, and C. Melodically as well as rhythmically the superius is clearly the most important part, delivering the text in a predominantly syllabic fashion. The contratenor, however, is also supplied with text, singing the phrases missing from the superius. This practice of dividing a lengthy text between two or more voices so that different portions of it are sung at the same time is known as 'telescoping'; it occurs in several of the Gloria and Credo settings in the Old Hall manuscript and was presumably intended to keep such settings from being excessively long.

TRANSLATION
For a translation, see No. 11k.

67. Beata progenies

Votive antiphon in English descant style   Lionel Power (c.1370–1445)

32 Counter: MS. 'quem'   33 Tenor: MS. breve

GB–OH, 49.

This setting of an antiphon of the Virgin is taken from the Old Hall manuscript and is probably one of Power's earliest compositions, being stylistically similar to the anonymous Sanctus (No. 64). It is a typical English descant piece (an important class of composition in the Old Hall MS): the plainsong is presented as the middle of three voices in an unornamented form; the voices move mainly in note-against-note counterpoint; the descant and counter move largely in contrary motion. Comparison of this composition with a Credo by Power from the same source (No. 66) will give some idea of Power's wide stylistic range.

TRANSLATION

O blessed stock from which Christ was born: how glorious is the virgin who gave birth to the King of Heaven.

68. Se je souspir

Virelai   Guillaume de Machaut (c.1300–1377)

Us–NYw 91, F–Pn 1584 97, Pn 22546 98.

The *virelai* was one of the favourite formes fixes among French composers of the Ars Nova. It consisted of two musical units (a and b). A textual refrain was sung to the first unit and this was followed by the stanza, which consisted of several lines sung to two statements of the second unit followed by further lines sung to the first unit, after which the refrain was repeated. The musical form was thus AbbaA. Further stanzas would extend the form to AbbaAbbaA, etc. Thirty-two virelais by Machaut are preserved, and this is one of the most remarkable. Noteworthy are the interaction of the voices, with the duplum beginning below the tenor, the cadence on a third in the ouvert ending of the b section, the staggered phrases and the unusual textual grouping of eight- and four-syllable lines. Whereas the lives of most medieval composers are enveloped in obscurity, a great deal is known about Machaut's biography, with the exception of his birth-date. As secretary to King John of Luxembourg he travelled widely with his royal patron between 1323 and 1330, and during this period he was awarded several religious benefices including a canonry at Rheims. After the death of John in 1346 Machaut served under his daughter, Bonne, and later under King Charles of Navarre, King Charles V of France and Pierre de Lusignan, King of Cyprus. In his book *Machaut* (OUP) Gilbert Reaney has formulated a chronology of Machaut's compositions.

TRANSLATION

If I sigh deeply and weep tenderly in secret, it is – upon my word – for you when, my lady, I do not see your shapely, lovely form. Your sweet bearing, simple and shy, your beautiful disposition, charming and pleasing, your fearless manner – these three have conquered me so sweetly that most lovingly I give myself wholly to you and surrender my heart, which in your absence neither beats nor rejoices.

If I sigh deeply and weep tenderly in secret, it is – upon my word – for you when, my lady, I do not see your shapely, lovely form.

69. J'aim la flour

Lai   Guillaume de Machaut (*c*.1300–1377)

85: F for D first time 86 C to 88 G all a third higher first time 127: G for third A

Paris, Bibliothèque National, MS fr. 9221, ff. 110r–111r.

The poetic and musical form of the *Lai* was related to that of the *Sequence* (see No. 11). Like its sacred counterpart, it consisted of a number of stanzas, usually grouped in pairs, while each group of stanzas had its own melody which was repeated for each stanza in the group. The lai was one of the most extended vernacular forms cultivated by the trobadors and trouvères; the examples by Machaut represent a final flowering of the genre before it passed from common usage. Trobador and trouvère lais frequently have a narrative function, but Machaut prefers more static and contemplative subject matter and, as in this example, often shows great skill in manipulating very restrictive rhyme schemes. All but three of

Machaut's 19 surviving lais are monophonic; in fact, with the exception of plainsong, the lai was the last important genre of the Middle Ages to attract monophonic composition. This example is relatively short and melodically simple; other examples by Machaut, for example *Ne say commencier*, are considerably longer and more elaborate. As in some sequences, *J'aim la flour* ends with the same melody as that with which it began.

TRANSLATION

I love that worthy flower which has no blemish, and adore her ardently night and day; for none is more worthy to be honoured for her warmth, colour, sweetness, and perfume; thus, languishing, I am willing to die for her love.

When I see the look in her eyes – which God preserve – through its magic my heart burns early and late, and she shoots a dart at me which may not be removed. Then I go away to another place, careless of whether I have any particle of joy, and so my heart breaks.

It is Love which leads me to this pass, just like anybody who seeks any happiness, and so he schools my heart, which finds no pleasure in anything; for relentlessly she torments me day and night and so repays me that, indeed, I believe that she is destroying me without good reason.

For Love bears down upon me and in my languor I can find no help for my sadness against Love. Whence come my dolorous sufferings, full of tears, and they are always very great in many ways, and it is fear which causes me all these pains.

For through fear of being rejected I dare not tell my lady that I live in torment for love of her, because if she were to turn against me or deny me my heart would certainly at once die of grief.

Nevertheless, I will love her with heart and soul as my sovereign lady, without thinking to criticize her or say evil things about her, however true it may be that she enflames my heart with that amorous passion, and starves it in her prison night and day.

However, if I can, when I see her I will tell her of the burden that I bear. Alas, I will not do it; instead I will keep silent and wait composedly to see what she does; although I am in great trouble and dismay on her account, yet I will do it, and so I shall never be light-hearted, but shall die for her whom I love so loyally.

And, if I can remain in her favour, know truly that I shall always obey her sweet command, to the best of my ability, night and day, without deceit and with a humble heart; for if I serve her loyally and in hope, I trust that she will understand and appreciate that I can have neither reward nor my desire without her solace.

Love, you know well that I am hers and wholly yours. Now you have bound me in your bonds, and you do not wish her to know anything of it; and you do not permit any happiness to be mine. You keep me a prisoner by your tricks, and so I die if you are not merciful to me.

Even if she has my heart, as I concede she has, I must ask no respite, except from you, for the sharp pain that I suffer; for when I see her sweet face and must tell her that in good faith I love her, I get myself into such a state that I dare not speak to her.

I bewail this bitterly and sigh deeply, when at length and leisure I gaze on the great beauty of her rosy face which I have loved so long, I dare not confess to her or reveal how I am condemned to languish and, in languishing, to die for her whom I love so greatly.

Alas, at least if she knew of my suffering and acknowledged it, she would surely harm me but little and comfort me much in my sad fate, and my death would not displease me if it pleased her; my heart would rather rejoice in it since it might thus obey her will.

Through its vehemence, the ardour which increases my weeping diminishes my strength. Alas, so I weep alone, without a resting place, and thus repose myself in such a way as to hope for no respite from death, through my timidity, for it is death which ends my grief.

Alas, alas, thus I groan and tremble, since I have not even half the name of lover; and my heart which has served her faithfully breaks in two; and I too, who in an evil hour saw her beauty, die unrequited, for which I humbly thank her.

70. Sans cuer/Amis, dolens/Dame, par vous

Canonic ballade   Guillaume de Machaut (*c.*1300–1377)

qui me de — — meu — re.

En lieu du cuer, da — me, qui vous de — — meu — re.

F–Pn 9221 57, F–Pn 1584 44, F–Pn 1586 21, F–Pn 22546 43, US–NYw 51.

During Machaut's lifetime the ballade became the most popular of the formes fixes, and settings of ballade texts could attain considerable size and complexity. The aab musical design of the ballade had frequently occurred in the trouvère repertory. The present example is Machaut's only known canonic ballade, although there is another tritextual (or triple) ballade by him. The first text is the lover's complaint, the second text is the lady's reassuring reply, and the third text is the lover's more hopeful reaction.

TRANSLATION

I leave without my heart, grieving and in tears, filled with sighs and bereft of joy, kindled and inflamed with such ardent longing, sweet Lady, to see you again for a brief moment, that I could not survive without my

heart, or endure such hardships, did not hope make her abode within me, in place of my heart, lady, which stays in you.

Sorrowing friend, wretched and disconsolate, you go away from me and wish me to believe that your heart remains wholly within me. I certainly do believe it; I could not reward you with a gift so fine, and be able to give you, with every good wish, whatever desire in the world it may relish in place of your heart, friend, which stays with me.

Lady, I feel myself consoled by you for all the sorrows which I am accustomed to experience. Through you I am freed from all deprivation; because of you I can feel nothing which upsets me; because of you I am prompted to hope for whatever a true friend may desire. It is consolation, if I haven't it already, in place of my heart, lady, which lives in you.

71. Tant doulcement

Rondeau   Guillaume de Machaut (c.1300–1377)

1, 4, 7. Tant doul — — — ce — — — ment me sans em-
3. Ja - mais ne quier es - tre des-
5. Car tous biens m'est en ces - te

- pri
- pri
pri

37 Duplum: MS. ♯ before G   42—3 Duplum: quaver F for crotchet F

F–*Pn 9221* 15, *Pn 1584* 73, *Pn 1586* 30, *Pb 22546* 80, *GB– Cmc 1594* 3, *US–NYpm 396* 5, *NYw* 79.

This rondeau shows Machaut's style at its most advanced and refined. Written in the duple metre fashionable in France for much of Machaut's career, it interweaves three non-blending lines over a supporting tenor. Rhythmic interest is created by syncopating one or more of the voices for several bars at a time, and quickly-resolving dissonances are frequently used for decorative purposes. Comparison of this piece with No. 56 (written probably less than a century earlier) will demonstrate the magnitude of the advances made in the Ars Nova period.

TRANSLATION

So sweetly I feel imprisoned that never did lover have so sweet a prison. Never do I seek to be released, so sweetly do I feel imprisoned. For in this prison every good thing has happened to me that a lady can give without dishonour. *So sweetly . . .*

72. Tres dous compains

Chace   Anonymous (French, mid-14th century)

I–IV 64.

Apart from Machaut's interpolations of chaces (canons) à 3 in his *Lai de la fonteine*, only four chaces have come down to us. All of them differ from their Italian counterparts in the absence of a tenor part supporting the canonic voices. The present example is a dawn song or aubade (compare the Provençal *alba*), and abounds in onomatopoeic sounds representing musical instruments, thus anticipating the programme chansons of the 15th century. Intentionally comic, it skilfully presents a hilarious vignette of peasant life. Although we print a three-part realization of this chace, there is some evidence that a two-part version only was intended; it will be seen that most of the dissonances are caused by the third voice. A performance might end at bar 71 or bar 81.

TRANSLATION

Sweet friend, get up, for I can sleep no longer, and only toss about; so I pray that we go immediately and play an estampie in front of my sweetheart's house. What is more I beg you, for love's sake, that we take, all of us in the party, little drums and bagpipes, lutes and great big flutes.

Let's both go back immediately and look for the trumpeters. They have all got up in a great hurry and, except for these two, gone off somewhere else to greet the morning. Come on, now, everybody, without any more interruptions! My dear friend, you begin the dance and we will follow along after you. Arrange yourselves properly! Come on, trumpeters: Blow! 'Po-po . . .' Quickly: 'Po-po . . .' God, what a fine time we're having! 'Ba-ba . . .' The drums have come. Ready now! 'Ton-ti-ti . . .' Now the bagpipe: 'Cu-re-lu-re . . .' The instruments are tuned. Ready, fifes! Fifes, play! 'Li-ri-li . . .' The morning is ours. It is time to go back now, my Lady, if it pleases you, for it is full daylight. Now, let's keep together and we'll go off and enjoy ourselves.

73. Sus une fontayne

Virelai in 'mannered' style   Johannes Ciconia (*c.*1335–1411)

I–MOe 5.24 48 ; GB–Ob 229 11.

This is a typical example of the 'mannered' chanson of the late 14th century. It is a composition of extreme rhythmic complexity, in which changes of metre and chains of syncopations occur without respite. Frequently three different mensurations operate at once, causing – at any rate for modern performers – acute problems of ensemble. Originally from Liège (where he was born in about 1335) Ciconia studied for the priesthood at Avignon and became a member of Cardinal Albornoz's retinue when it left for Italy in 1358. Ciconia journeyed again to Italy in 1366 and remained there until his death in December 1411. In spite of the technical dexterity which he displays in this example, Ciconia did not often compose in the 'mannered' style.

TRANSLATION

Under a spring gazing, I hear singing so sweet that my heart, my body, and my mind are seized, while awaiting solace for my sorrow which sharply pierces my heart. Alone seeing this noble flower which sang so sweetly, I know nothing subject as I am to fear, tremor and anguish. I must certainly do something, so much I desire to see her. Under a spring gazing, I hear singing so sweet that my heart, my body, and my mind are seized, while waiting.

74. Amor mi fa cantar

Ballata Anonymous (Italian, early 14th century)

I–*Rvat 215* 21.

The scarcity of Italian polyphony before 1300 is difficult to explain, considering the contribution made by this part of Europe to other artistic media. It may be that sources of Italian ars antiqua polyphony remain still to be discovered. At any rate, Italian musical life during the Ars Nova is much better documented, and it is clear that in the fourteenth century Italy witnessed in music as in other arts a creative flowering scarcely paralleled in other countries. The composition of music was encouraged by advances in musical notation, such as those described by Marchettus of Padua in his treatise *Pomerium* of 1314, which made possible the precise recording of a much wider range of rhythmic figures. Italian ars nova composers, of whom Francesco Landini and Jacopo da Bologna are the most famous, resembled their French contemporaries in setting mainly secular texts in the vernacular. Their output of secular songs falls into three categories – the *madrigal*, the *ballata*, and the *caccia*. The madrigal was most popular among the earlier fourteenth-century composers; it normally consisted of two three-line stanzas or *terzetti*, both set to the same music, and a concluding couplet called a *ritornello*, set to new material. The ballata replaced the madrigal in popularity towards the end of the century; it had the same musical form as the French virelai, consisting of a refrain or *ripresa* (A) flanking a number of stanzas, each of which was composed of two *piedi* sung to new music (bb) and a *volta* sung to the refrain music (a). The verse

exemplifies a common variant of the ballata form, in which the refrain A is heard only at the beginning and end, the stanzas following straight on from one another. Far fewer examples of the caccia survive. In contrast to the more introspective madrigal and ballata this was a genre full of excitement, employing canon and dealing with any episode which lent itself to vivid description. Many Italian songs of the Ars Nova are in two voices, with a rhythmically elaborate superius, rather less jagged and halting than in contemporary French music, over a more slowly moving supporting tenor. Both parts are usually texted. This duo is sometimes joined by a contratenor which in style is usually similar to the superius.

The manuscript from which this example is taken (the Rossi manuscript) is the earliest known collection of Italian secular polyphony, but all the ballate which it contains are monophonic.

'Amor mi fa cantar a la Francescha' is a pun: 'Love makes me sing to Francesca' and 'Love makes me sing in the French style'.

TRANSLATION

Love makes me sing to Francesca. Why this happens to me I dare not say, for she is that lady who makes me languish. I fear she would not come to dance with me. I am resolved to hide my heart from her and, rather, waste away for love of her, for at least I die for a noble object. Ladies, I can truly say this much, that this lady for whom I weep and sing is like a soft, fresh rose amid thorns. Love makes me sing to Francesca.

75. E con chaval

Madrigal   Anonymous (Italian, early 14th century)

45 Tenor: MS. semibreve for minim

I–*OST* 7.

In the ars nova madrigal each stanza of text is set to the same music, and there is sometimes (although not in this example) a second musical unit, usually in a different metre, called a *ritornello*. The two-part texture of *E con chaval,* with a florid vocal line moving chiefly by step above a supporting lower part, is typical of secular polyphony in the Italian Ars Nova. The organization of this piece is rather unusual. The tenor consists of six varied statements of a basic melodic pattern (compare bars 5–23 with bars 24–42), while the superius may be analysed as having three varied statements of the same melody material and an eight-bar conclusion. This piece is possibly the earliest known Italian composition using the ostinato technique.

The text appears to be in a Venetian dialect.

TRANSLATION

Count Hugo is out riding along the road when all of a sudden he meets a certain Ermengarda, the daughter of his lord. He throws an arm around her neck and kisses her with love, crying 'O Lord God, thou makest Ermengarda, thou who makest the moon and the sun.'

76. Aquila altera/Creatura gentile/Uccel di Dio

Madrigal with ritornello Jacopo da Bologna (mid–14th century)

I–*Fn 26* 163, I–*Fl 87* 14, F–*Pn 6771* 3, F–*Pn 568* 2.

In this tritextual madrigal the imitative opening and the imitation starting at bar 30 join with recurring rhythmic patterns in producing a distinctly unified composition. The contratenor is not relegated to a subordinate role, but actually participates with the superius in the manner of a duet, while the tenor adheres to a supporting function. Jacopo was active in the middle of the 14th century. It is known that he was in the service of Lucchino Visconti in Milan in about 1346, and in about 1349 he was at the court of Can Grande della Scala in Verona. There he engaged in musical contests with the earliest Italian trecento composer, Magister Piero.

TRANSLATION

Superius: Lofty eagle, gazing with valiant eye upon the summit of that noble mind where your life finds its repose! Therein is semblance, therein is true bliss.

Contratenor: O noble creature, O being worthy to ascend on high, to gaze upon the sun is uniquely what your nature wills! Therein lies the image,

therein is perfection.

Tenor: Bird of God, banner of the just, you possess above all else radiant glory, for in great deeds do you triumph! Therein I saw the shadow, therein the true essence.

77. L'alma mia piange

Ballata   **Francesco Landini** (*c.*1325–1397)

41 Followed by whole bar's rest in MSS.

I–*Fn 26* 60, I–*Fl 87* 186, GB–*Lbm 29987* 106, F–*Pn 568* 90.

Although the melodic interest in this ballata is centered on the cantus line, the contratenor and tenor occasionally exchange their supporting roles for a more melodic one, as in bars 4–8. Noteworthy is the sequential writing in the superius in bars 23–28, the imitation between superius and contratenor in bars 42–45, and the parallel 6/3 chords at the end of each section. More music survives by Landini than by any of his Italian contemporaries. Most of his compositions are secular songs, but fragments of a few motets also survive, suggesting that perhaps the motet was not as uncommon in 14th-century Italy as is often thought. Blinded in youth by smallpox, Landini was organist at the church of San Lorenzo in Florence.

TRANSLATION

My soul weeps and can find no peace, since you have deprived me, Lady, of the fair sight with which you enflamed me. The sweet vision was of such delight that I fell in love at the first glance from you, hoping to obtain that blessing that derives so often from loving. Yet I see my hopes fading, for you will not raise your face to me, and here am I in woe and tribulation. My soul weeps and can find no peace, since you have deprived me, Lady, of the fair sight with which you enflamed me.

78. Fa metter bando

Madrigal **Francesco Landini** (*c*.1325-1397)

1. Fa, fa met-ter ban-do et co-man-da-r'a-mo-re,
2. Et, et che ni-un si ri-man-ga d'a-ma-re,
3. Et, et che ni-u-n'a-man-te si di-spe-ri

a, ccia-sche du-n'a-man-ça o ve-r'a-man-te Ce-la-to ten-gha in fat-t'e in sen-bian-
Per, per-ch'al lui non pa-ia es-ser can-bia-to C'a-mor vuol che chi a-ma si a-ma-
Per, per lun-g'a-mar che giu-gnen-do a gli ef-fet-to gni sua pe-na tor-ne-ra in di-let-

13 Cantus: MS. AA for GG

I–Fl *87* 169; Fn *26* 78.

The melodic contour and rhythmic articulation of the upper voice of this madrigal are unusually subtle even for the fastidious Landini. The balance between animation and relaxation is carefully planned; effective sequential writing occurs between bars 27 and 31; and the anticipation at bars 55–56 of the closing motive adds to the weight of the final cadence. Note also the careful balancing of phrase lengths in the upper voice, and the brief initial imitation between the voices.

TRANSLATION

Let it be proclaimed and decreed by Love that every lover and sweetheart should hide his true feelings in his behaviour and bearing.

And that nobody should cease to love because he does not seem to be reciprocated; for Love desires that he who loves should be loved.

And that no lover should despair at loving for a long time, for when he achieves his desire every pain will be turned into delight.

Let it be known that whoever breaks this law will be deprived of love if he does not mend his ways.

79. Povero çappator

Isorhythmic madrigal   Lorenzo da Firenze (*fl. c.*1370)

13 and 26 Followed by whole bar's rest in MSS.   21 Both MSS. corrupt. Reading based on Lbm 29987

I–Fl 87 78, GB–Lbm 29987 49.

The principle of isorhythmic organization was not unknown in 14th-century Italy, although only very few Italian isorhythmic compositions are known to exist. The music for the two stanzas of this madrigal is constructed on a thrice-stated thirteen-bar tenor talea, while the superius is not strictly isorhythmic. Note that the third bar of the tenor talea is a repetition in diminution of the first two bars. The ritornello is also isorhythmic, having a new tenor talea which is subjected to proportional treatment.

Lorenzo is mentioned as a composer by the 14th-century historian Villani, who also says that his surname was Masini. In Lbm 29987 he is listed as 'Ser Lorenzo da Firenze, prete' (priest). Seventeen of his compositions are known – ten madrigals, five ballatas, one caccia, and a Sanctus.

TRANSLATION

A poor tiller of the soil, I am brought by an abandoned ship, tossed by the sea which I have left behind me. And that planet which brings good fortune [Venus] is guiding it to its destination, but I do not see that it is nearing its journey's end to bring me aid. As I wait, my strength fails, and I feed on grief, renewing my suffering.

80. Dappoi che'l sole

Caccia   Niccolò da Perugia (later 14th century)

I–*Fl 87 98*, GB–*Lbm 29987 57*.

The *caccia* (a 'chase', hence a canon) was in sharp contrast to the more introspective madrigal. Any scene lending itself to a vivid description was used as subject matter, hunting topics and the cries of itinerant vendors being especially popular. This example deals with the hustle and bustle of a fire, and, like all pieces in the genre, abounds in cries, commands, onomatopoeic effects, and the like. Noteworthy is the metaphor in the ritornello, linking the all-consuming fire with the appearance of Cicilia, the poet's devouring passion. The two canonic voices are supported by a more slowly moving tenor line. Little is known of Niccolò. Presumably from Perugia, he was attracted to Florence and there composed many madrigals, ballatas, and cacce, several being on texts by Franco Sacchetti. One of his earliest compositions is the madrigal *Come selvaggia fera* (1354). He was still alive in 1400, for his *La fiera testa* alludes to the powerful and aggressive Milanese leader Giangaleazzo Visconti, whose forces occupied Perugia from 1400 to 1402.

TRANSLATION

The sun was hiding its sweet rays and the moon poured forth its splendour, when I heard a great noise and cries of 'Fire, fire, fire!' Then, after a moment, 'Where is it, where is it?' 'It's here!' 'Come, come, every man, come!' 'Bring light!' 'Out with the lamps and the lanterns!' 'You with the bell, ring out!' 'Ding, dong, ding, dong.' 'Sound the alarm!' 'Here, you, take this helmet, this axe and this gorget!' 'Hurry, hurry, for the fire is spreading!' 'Send for the servants!' 'Water, water, up with the jugs!' Some bought ewers, some ladders, and some were hurt. And some shouted: 'Hurry, help me!' 'You with the trumpet, blow!' 'Ta-ta, ta-ta!' 'Step back!' Some scampered away and some looted while others poured water, and one smashed at the door with a hatchet. Here everyone was hurrying intent on smothering the fire and the sparks. The sound of alarm-bells had died away when the ringers shouted: 'To your homes, everybody, for the fire is out!' Turning, I saw the one who is always in my heart – C I C I with L with I and A.

81. Serà quel zorno

Ballata **Matteo da Perugia (late 14th–early 15th century)**

Pren - da el ____ mio cor che vi - ve in tan - ti gua ___
Per te ____ si stru - ze et man - ca in pian - ti O - ma ___

____ mio cor che vi - ve in tan - ti gua ___
____ si stru - ze et man - ca in pian - ti O - ma ___

___ ___ ___ ___ i, che vi - ve in ___ tan - ti gua ___
___ ___ ___ ___ i, et man - ca in ___ pian - ti O - ma ___

___ ___ ___ ___ i, che vi - ve in tan - ti gua ___
___ ___ ___ ___ i, et man - ca in pian - ti O - ma ___

___ ___ i? ____ 2. Cer ___ ___ ___ ___
___ ___ i? ____ 3. Ne ___

___ ___ i? ____ 2. Cer ___ ___ ___ ___
___ ___ i? ____ 3. Ne ___

- to ___ non ___ ben con - ven ___ ___ ___ ___ ___
che in ___ sum - ma bel - tà ___

- to non ben ___ con - ven ___ ___ ___ ___
che in sum - ma ___ bel - tà ___

I–MOe 5.24 97.

Abounding in syncopation, rhythmic repetition, snatches of imitation, and chains of descending 6/3 chords, this composition is typical of late ars nova ballate. The textless contratenor, with its many wide leaps, was probably performed on an instrument. Little is known of Matteo's life apart from his service as a singer in the choir of Milan cathedral between 1402 and 1407 and between 1414 and 1416. About thirty of his compositions have been preserved. They include settings of French and Italian secular lyrics and five polyphonic Glorias.

TRANSLATION

Will the day ever dawn, my sweet lady, when you will graciously accept my heart which suffers so much pain? It is not fitting that so noble a being should be devoid of pity, nor that such beauty should lack courtesy towards my wretched spirits which are set on fire. Do you not see that my heart is consumed for you and pines away in tears? Will the day ever dawn, my sweet lady, when you will graciously accept my heart which suffers so much pain?

82. O Virgo splendens

Caça   **Anonymous (Spanish, 14th century)**

E–MO11.

The *caca* is the Spanish counterpart of the Italian caccia and the French chace. This example from the *Llibre Vermell,* a fourteenth-century manuscript kept at the monastery of Monserrat in Catalonia, is written in a non-mensural notation, to which we have given our own rhythmic interpretation. Unusually, the ligatures seem to have no mensural significance, but, as quite often in late medieval music, they serve to indicate the textual underlay.

TRANSLATION

O resplendent Virgin, here on the miraculous mountain cleft everywhere by dazzling wonders, and which all of the faithful climb. Behold with the merciful eye of love those enmeshed in the bonds of sin, that they will not have to endure the blows of hell, but rather will be named among the blessed through your intercession.

83. Stella splendens

Polyphonic pilgrim song with tornada   Anonymous (Spanish, 14th century)

E–MO1 2.

Another composition from the *Llibre Vermell*, this pilgrim song has a *tornada* or refrain which is sung after each of the twenty-four stanzas. The melody has a distinctly popular character, while the straightforward rhythmic style is appropriate for processional singing.

Only one stanza is printed here.

TRANSLATION

O star, shining like a ray of the sun on the mountain miraculously cleft, hear your people.

All of the people come rejoicing, rich and poor, great and small.

They climb the mountain so that their eyes see, and return thence filled with grace.

O star . . .

84. Estampie

Composition for keyboard instrument   Anonymous (? English, *c.*1325)

Secundus punctus

Tertius punctus

Quartus punctus

76-7 Left hand: G for A

GB–*Lbm* Arundel 28550 f. 43.

This is one of several compositions contained in the earliest known example of keyboard notation, four leaves, dating from about 1325, bound among non-musical material relating to Robertsbridge Abbey in Sussex. The music on the top stave is copied in conventional ars nova musical notation which is rather Italianate in style, while the music on the bottom stave is notated alphabetically. Alphabetic notation, sometimes combined with conventional note-symbols, is commonly found in German sources of fifteenth- and sixteenth-century keyboard music, such as the Buxheim organ book. This estampie consists of four puncti, the first of which is supplied with ouvert and clos endings. The performer is directed to repeat the final section of the first punctus after puncti II, III, and IV. The music is mainly in two parts, with a middle voice added here

and there for extra sonority. Two manuscript signs, □ and ○, seem to indicate some kind of ornamentation. A correct performance of the piece will take the following form:

Punctus I (Bars 1–39+*overt* ending)
Punctus I repeated (Bars 1–39+*clos* ending)
Punctus II played twice (Bars 47–62)
Punctus I (Bars 8–39+*clos* ending)
Punctus III played twice (Bars 63–82)
Punctus I (Bars 8–39+*clos* ending)
Punctus IV played twice (Bars 83–107)
Punctus I (Bars 8–39+*clos* ending)

To shorten the piece it would be possible to omit the repetition of Puncti II, III, and IV.

85. Aquila altera

Instrumental transcription of madrigal   Anonymous (Italian, early 15th century)

Aquila altera

Volta de aquila latera

I–*Fzc 117* f. 73.

This instrumental arrangement of a madrigal by Jacopo da Bologna (see No. 76) comes from the Faenza codex, one of the earliest complete sources of instrumental music. The Faenza codex was copied between about 1410 and 1420, but the compositions upon which the transcriptions are based date from the second half of the fourteenth century. The contents of the manuscript have usually been taken to be keyboard music, but the frequent crossing of parts and duplication of notes on both staves (as here in bar 48) suggests that in some cases the use of two melody instruments might be appropriate. In the Faenza transcriptions of two-part vocal pieces the lower part usually adheres to the lower voice of the original while the upper part elaborates the vocal superius. In transcriptions of three-part compositions the higher instrumental line usually draws on the superius and contratenor of the vocal original.

86. Chominciamento di gioia

Istampita   Anonymous (Italian, 14th century)

From bar 63 to bar 88D the MS. gives the melody a third higher than printed.

107: crotchet D after second F

GB–*Lbm* 29987, f. 56.

Boccaccio's *Decamerone* and Prodenzani's *Il Sollazzo* both mention the *istampita* or estampie being played in front of guests, but in neither case do the guests arise to dance. It would seem, therefore, that in fourteenth-century Italy the instrumental istampita sometimes lost its practical function and became absolute music, intended to be listened to rather than to be danced. This example is one of several in the same source to bear a fanciful title – others are *Isabella*, *Tre Fontane*, and *Parlamento*. The istampita falls into several sections or puncti – five in this case – which may repeat and be provided with *aperto* and *chiuso* endings, equivalent to our first-time and second-time bars. The five puncti of *Chominciamento di gioia* all end in the same way, a fact indicated in the manuscript by a rather involved system of signs. In some places the notation is ambiguous.

87. Salterello

Instrumental dance **Anonymous (Italian, 14th century)**

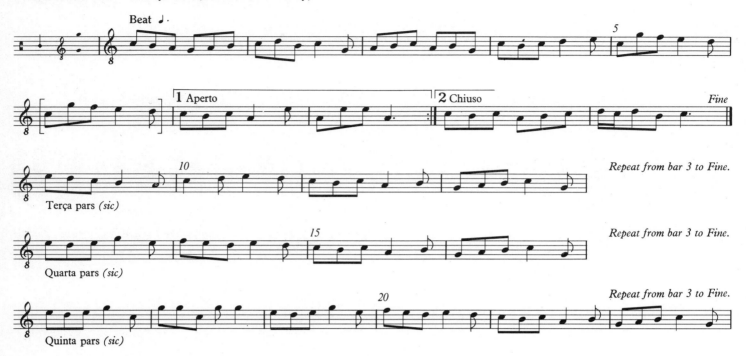

GB–*Lbm 29987*, ff. 62v–63r.

The saltarello (the spelling of the title is that of the manuscript) was a popular Italian dance executed with leaps and skips, although no details of its choreography are known. This example is in the form of an istampita or estampie – a series of sections or puncti, each repeated and supplied with aperto and chiuso endings. Bar 6 of our transcription is not given in the source; we have repeated the melody of bar 5 in order to fill out what seems to be an incomplete phrase-length.

The Fifteenth Century

88. Telus purpurium/Splendida flamigero/*Tenor*

Isorhythmic motet **John Benet** (*fl.*1430–50)

75 Triplum: E for D   104 Superius: G for first F

Modena, Biblioteca Estense, α.X.1.11, ff. 125v–126r (128v–129r).

The decline in popularity experienced by the isorhythmic motet during the first half of the 15th century may be partly explained by the emergence of the *cyclic mass*, a genre which allowed musical construction on just as large a scale while freeing the composer from the limiting factors inherent in isorhythmic design. During the Ars Nova period the continental isorhythmic motet had become a largely secular and ceremonial genre; in England, however, it had retained much of its originally sacred character, although it may well have been performed outside a liturgical context. This example by John Benet is isorhythmic in all its voices. The tenor, whose source has not been identified, is treated *proportionally*, being restated in note values reduced successively by one third and two thirds. The texts are in honour of St Alban.

TRANSLATION

Triplum: The earth gave birth to a purple flower of the British race which like a heavenly star gives its light everywhere. This is the blessed Alban, flower of the faith and rose of the world; and a violent hand shed waves of his blood. Lying prone while the light falls, the first martyr dies and in doing so gives a light to the people. He dries up the river, feeling pity for the people passing, so that the divine will and truth should prevail together. At the top of the hill a stream quickly flows and by a springing wave gives a healing draught. Now, soldier of Christ, protect the camp of your servants and, rescuing us from a doleful death, lead us, O martyr, to the starts.

Motetus: A splendid shining light blazed from a fiery star when in martyrdom he held up the palm of faith. He sowed a new seed on the hard earth for the citizens and nurtured his own hungry race. Hear this in your praise when we rejoice with song. And be a kind father of the English and a leader of your people.

89. Kyrie

Polyphonic mass movement   Guillaume Dufay (*c.*1400–1474)

Bologna, Liceo G. B. Martini, MS Q.15, ff. 164v–165; Cambrai, Bibliothèque de la Ville, MS 6, 3, MS 11, 3; Aosta, Seminary Library, MS without shelf number, 26, 46; Munich Staatsbibliothek, Mus. MS. 3232a, 55; Venice, Biblioteca Marciana, MS It. IX, 145. f. 2v.

This example comes from a Kyrie-Gloria-Credo setting whose movements are not, as they would be in a true cyclic mass, musically interrelated. The music probably dates from the early 1420s; it shows, perhaps even more clearly in the Gloria and Credo which are not printed here, the influences of Dufay's immediate predecessors such as Richard Loqueville, who was Master of the choristers at Cambrai Cathedral while Dufay was a chorister there.

The style is basically that of the solo song, 'treble-dominated', with the tenor and contratenor supplying a harmonic support. There is, however, rather more melodic equality among the voices than is usual, and we have added text (breaking some ligatures in the process) to make possible an entirely vocal performance.

TRANSLATION
For a translation of the text, see No. 11b.

90. *Agnus Dei from Mass* Salve Sancta parens

Movement from cyclic mass **Anonymous (English, *c.*1435)**

13 Contratenor primus: D is dotted

26 Contratenor primus: B for C   32 Contratenor secundus: semibreve for minim   41 Contratenor primus: C for D

53 Contratenor primus E for D.   71 Contratenor primus: G for F   72 Contratenor primus: F for E

Trent, Castello del Buon Consiglio, MS 90, ff. 232v–234r; MS 93, ff. 301v–303r.

In 14th-century polyphonic settings of the Ordinary of the Mass the individual movements were musically unrelated to each other. In the early 15th century, however, a new type of polyphonic Ordinary appeared in which the movements – Kyrie, Gloria, Credo, Sanctus, and Agnus Dei – were related to each other by sharing musical material or (less often) by the consistent application of a certain technical device, such as canon. This new genre is called the *cyclic mass*. English composers seem to have played a major role in its creation, possibly because of the experience which they had gained in setting mass texts throughout the 14th century, at a time when continental composers had rarely set them. Several of the mass movements in the 'Fountains fragment' and the 'Old Hall' manuscript are based on isorhythmic tenors, and it was through an extension of this idea that English composers created their first cyclic masses. In these each movement is based on the same tenor melody which is usually taken from the plainsong repertory, and the resulting cycle is known as a *tenor mass*. Sometimes the rhythmic disposition of the tenor is the same in every movement, as in the present example. At other times

the rhythm of the tenor changes from one movement to another and the tenor melody may be ornamented in varied ways, as in the Mass *Rex saeculorum* attributed to both Lionel Power and John Dunstable. The earliest English cyclic masses, such as Power's Mass *Alma redemptoris mater* of about 1425, were in three voices with a melodic superius above a supporting tenor-contratenor duet. Four-voice settings began to appear slightly later, from about 1435 onwards, the extra voice usually being a *contratenor bassus* lying mainly below the tenor. Early cyclic masses were composed for performance on very important occasions, thus taking over some of the ceremonial functions of the isorhythmic motet. They normally included a setting of a troped Kyrie (the Mass *Salve sancta parens* has a setting of the English trope *Deus Creator*). Because a trope made a Kyrie part of the Proper rather than part of the Ordinary, polyphonic settings of Kyrie tropes seem to have been copied into manuscripts detached from the other movements with which they formed a cycle. As a result many of them have been partially or wholly lost, and this has given rise to the mistaken impression that in the early days of the cyclic mass the Kyrie was not set.

TRANSLATION

For a translation, see No. 119.

91. *Gloria from Mass* Sine nomine

Movement from cyclic mass   Jean Pullois (*c.*1430–1478)

1 Superius follows *Tr. 90*

35 Contratenor: D for E   62 Superius: B for A

83 Superius follows *Tr. 90* 93 Contratenor: B for second C 94—5 Tenor: ED for FE 101 Contratenor: C for D 118 Superius: E for D

170 Tenor: G for A

Trent, Castello del Buon Consiglio, MS 87, ff. 168v–170r; MS 90, 105v–107r; Prague, Strahov MS, ff. 147v–148v.

English music was extremely popular in France and northern Italy during the first half of the 15th century, and continental composers sought to reproduce its sonority and consonance in their own music. They also took up the cyclic mass. In the cycle from which this Gloria is taken the rhythmic organization of the tenor varies from movement to movement

and the tenor melody (untraced, hence the title *Sine nomine*) is decorated with considerable freedom. The superius begins each movement with the same short melodic phrase or *head motive*, a device often used further to unify a Mass cycle. From 1447 until his death Pullois was a member of the Papal choir. This must be one of his early compositions.

TRANSLATION

For a translation, see No. 11c.

92. *Sanctus from Mass* Tubae

Movement from cyclic mass   Cousin (mid-15th century)

- - - - - - - ctus Do - mi - - - - - - - - - nus De - - us _____ Sa - ba - - - - - - - - - - - - - - - - - - - oth.

Tenor
tacet

54 Superius: minim E

Repeat *Hosanna in excelsis.*

83 Contratenor secundus: B for first C   80 Tenor: A for G

Trent, Castello del Buon Consiglio, MS 90, ff. 441v–443r.

The Mass *Tubae* by the little-known composer Cousin is an example of a cycle unified by the consistent application of a technique rather than by shared musical material. Throughout the mass the three lower voices spend most of their time in outlining triadic motives which, either because they were played on slide-trumpets (an ancestor of the trombone) or because they sounded as if they ought to be, gave the work its name. Supporting voices of this type are not uncommon in continental music of the earlier 15th century, occurring for instance in Dufay's well-known *Gloria ad modum tubae.*

TRANSLATION

For a translation, see No. 11n.

93. *Credo from Mass* Dueil angoisseus

Movement from cyclic mass   **John Bedyngham** (*fl.*1440–60)

5 Tenor follows Tr. 90   19 Contratenor: E for D   31 Superius: DC for CB

49—51 Superius follows Tr. 90

Trent, Castello del Buon Consiglio, MS 88, ff. 29v–31r; MS 90, ff. 386v–389r (four voices).

By the 1440s cyclic masses were being written on tenor cantus firmi taken from secular sources, especially from chansons. In his Mass *Dueil angoisseus* the English composer John Bedyngham subjects the tenor of a chanson by Binchois (see No. 100) to extremely free rhythmic and melodic variation. He also uses the opening of the chanson superius as a head motive. In some places, for instance between bars 41 and 59, the Credo is so closely based on all three voices of the original that the parody technique of the early 16th century is anticipated. The two sources of this movement frequently conflict in the text incipits which they give to the contratenor voice. The intention of *Tr* 90 seems to be to include as much of the Credo text as possible, sometimes altering the underlay of the superius in the process, whereas *Tr* 88 simply omits large portions of the text. The reader is at liberty to underlay the contratenor line for himself, filling out either set of incipits, or alternatively the part may be vocalized or played on an instrument.

TRANSLATION

For a translation, see No. 11k.

94. Magnificat

Canticle at Vespers　Anonymous (English, *c*.1430)

Ma - gni - fi - cat　a - ni - ma　me - a　Do - mi - num.

11 Discantus: B for first A　13 Discantus: A for first B

34–5 Discantus: BGABGC for AGBCAB   46 Discantus: G for second A   47 Discantus: BA for AG

Et mi-se-ri-cor-di-a e-ius a pro-ge-ni-e__ in__pro-ge-ni-es ti-men-ti-bus e-um.

50 Beat ♩ slightly slower than preceding ♩

Fe — cit__ po-ten-ti — — — — — am

Fe — cit__ po-ten-ti — — — — — am

Fe — cit po-ten-ti — — — — — am

in __ bra — chi — o su — — — — — — — — — — —

in ___ bra — chi — o __ su — — — — — — — —

in bra-chi — o su — — — — — — — — — — —

- o: dis — per-sit su — per — — bos men — —

- o:__ dis — per-sit su — per — — bos__ men — —

- o: dis — per-sit su — per — — bos men — —

- te __ cor — dis __ su — — — — — — — — — i.

- te__ cor — dis su — — — — — — — — i.

- te__ cor — dis su — — — — — — — — i.

De - po-su — it po-ten-tes__ de se — de, et ex-al-ta-vit hu-mi-les.

E - su — ri — en — tes im — ple — — — —

E - su — ri — en — tes__ im — ple — —

E - su — — ri — en — tes im — ple — — —

55 Contratenor: minim B, crotchet second D   64 Discantus: F for second G

91. Discantus: B for A   92–3 Discantus: EDBABCB for DCAGABA

Trent, Castello del Buon Consiglio, MS 87, ff. 81v–82v.

The composer of this anonymous Magnificat was almost certainly English. In the middle of the 14th century English composers began to set the Magnificat in polyphony – a procedure which did not become common the continent until the 1420s or 30s. The earliest English settings use one of the Magnificat reciting tones as a cantus firmus. During the 15th century, however, it became customary among English composers to employ as a cantus firmus not a Magnificat tone itself but a melody called a *faburden*. As far as is known, continental composers never adopted this approach. Faburden was an English method of 'harmonizing' a plainsong by improvising a contrapuntal line beneath it – a practice which extended back at least into the 14th century and which continued up until the Reformation. The present example is one of the earliest Magnificat settings to be based on a faburden melody, in this case the one associated with the eighth Magnificat tone. As in almost all later English settings, polyphony is provided only for the even-numbered verses and

the mensuration changes to *tempus imperfectum* for verses 6 and 8. We have supplied the plainsong for the odd-numbered verses from *The Use of Sarum,* vol. II, p. lxxj.

TRANSLATION

My soul doth magnify the Lord: and my spirit hath rejoiced in God my Saviour. For He hath regarded: the lowliness of His hand-maiden'. For behold, from henceforth: all generations shall call me blessed. For He that is mighty hath magnified me: and holy is His Name. And His mercy is on them that fear Him: throughout all generations. He hath shewed strength with His arm: He hath scatterèd the proud in the imagination of their hearts. He hath put down the mighty from their seat: and hath exalted the humble and meek. He hath filled the hungry with good things: and the rich He hath sent empty away. He remembering His mercy hath holpen His servant Israel: as He promised to our forefathers, Abraham and his seed for ever. Glory be to the Father, and to the Son: and to the Holy Ghost. As it was in the beginning, is now, and ever shall be: world without end. Amen.

95. Veni, Creator Spiritus

Hymn set in fauxbourdon   Gilles Binchois (*c*.1400–1460)

Trent, Castello del Buon Consiglio, MS 92, f. 25r.
Plainsong (for comparison) from *Hymnorum . . . Sarum* (J. Coccius, 1541), f. 57v.

The technique called *fauxbourdon* may well have been the invention of the Burgundian composer Guillaume Dufay (*c.*1400–1474); its first known appearances are in compositions by him which date from the late 1420s. In fauxbourdon a top part and a bottom part were written out in full, the former usually being a decorated version or *paraphrase* of a plainsong and the latter moving mainly in parallel sixths below it, descending to the octave at cadence points. A middle part was then improvised by singing in parallel fourths below the top voice. The result – a chain of 6/3 chords widening out to an 8/5 chord at the cadences – reproduced quite accurately the sound of a type of English composition known as the *cantilena*, and this may have been the purpose for which it was devised. Fauxbourdon was used most frequently for setting hymns. The *Veni Creator* plainsong is given to demonstrate how paraphrase was carried out.

TRANSLATION

Come, Holy Ghost, Creator blest, Vouchsafe within our souls to rest; Come with thy grace and heavenly aid, And fill the hearts which thou has made.

96. Quam pulchra es

Marian antiphon   John Pyamour (*fl.*1420–30)

3 Contratenor: *Tr. 92* has ♯ for C

43 Contratenor: *Tr. 92* has ♯ for C   53 Superius: *Tr. 92* 'floruissent'   54 Contratenor: F for first G   60 Superius: E for second D

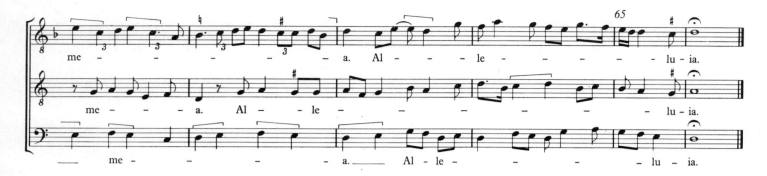

Modena, Biblioteca Estense, MS lat. 471 (*Mod B*), ff. 93v–94r (95v–96r); Trent, Castello del Buon Consiglio, MS 92, ff. 172v–173r. The music follows the former, the text mainly the latter.

The *Marian antiphon* was a devotional text, either taken from the liturgy or newly invented, which was sung in honour of the Virgin. Although non-liturgical, Marian antiphons were often sung in church after Compline, at first in plainsong settings but, during the late Middle Ages, with increasing frequency in polyphonic settings. Marian antiphons seem first to have been set in polyphony in England during the second half of the 14th century. Many of the earlier examples make use of the plainsong to which the text would otherwise have been sung, treating it either as a tenor cantus firmus or paraphrasing it in the superius. Continental composers did not begin to set Marian antiphons until the 1420s, when they took over the genre as part of their general admiration for English music. This example, by a composer who was a member of the Chapel Royal and later of the Chapel of the Duke of Bedford, is slightly unusual in being written in duple metre. Its sonority and melodic grace are typical of English music at this time, although the treatment of dissonance is not as disciplined as it would become in another ten or twenty years. The tenor may well be based on a plainsong, but this has not been traced.

TRANSLATION

How fair and how pleasant art thou, my dearest one, in thy charms! Thy tall figure is like to a palm tree, and thy breasts to clusters of grapes. Thine head upon thee is like Carmel; thy neck is as a tower of ivory. Come, my beloved, let us go forth into the field; let us see if the flowers will have borne fruit; if the pomegranates will have blossomed; there will I offer thee my breasts. Alleluia.

97. Speciosa facta es

Votive antiphon   John Dunstable (*c.*1390–*c.*1453)

Trent, Castello del Buon Consiglio, MS 92, ff. 180v–181r; Modena, Bibliotèca Estense, MS lat. 471 *(ModB)*, f. 100(A)v.

This setting of a processional antiphon of the Virgin does not make use of the plainsong. The smoothly flowing melodic line, the high degree of consonance and the emphasis on the 3rd and the 6th as vertical intervals are typical features in the music of Dunstable and his English contemporaries. The cadential ornament in bar 6 of the superius and the turning figure in superius bar 40 became 'fingerprints' in English music of Dunstable's generation, and melodies outlining triads (superius 43–4) are also common.

TRANSLATION

You are made beautiful and pleasant in the delights of virginity, O holy Mother of God, whom the daughters of Sion praised when they saw you and queens extolled as the most blessed one, flowering with roses and lilies of the valley.

98. Se cuer d'amant

Rondeau   Baude Cordier (*fl. c.*1400)

Bologna, Conservatorio G.B. Martini, MS Q 15 (*olim* Lic. Mus. 37), ff. 158v–159r.

This rondeau exemplifies the simpler sort of chanson being composed at the turn of the 14th century. The musical interest is clearly concentrated in the superius, which is the only voice to carry the full text. The tenor and contratenor form a supporting duo, the former being rather more 'finished' melodically and rhythmically than the latter. The introductory melisma may have been vocalized by the singer or played on an instrument. The tradition of the French chanson was kept alive in pieces of this unassuming type, rather than in complex and artificial compositions like No. 73; stylistically the latter turned out to be a dead end.

TRANSLATION

If a lover's heart, by humbling itself, can deserve solace despite the wrongs he has done, I believe that my peerless lady should release me from my sufferings. I do nothing but grow melancholy, but nevertheless I must not be blamed. If a lover's heart . . . he has done. For indeed we see the greatest men acting foolishly sometimes, even the wisest of them, so, since I am only a prisoner, I am in a much better position to say, without getting it wrong: If a lover's heart . . . from my sufferings.

99. Belle, veullies moy retenir (opposite)
Oxford, Bodleian Library, MS Canonici Misc 213, f. 51v.

This early rondeau by Dufay probably dates from the late 1420s. The 9/8 rhythm of the superius was popular among French composers during the first quarter of the 15th century, but virtually disappeared during the 1430s, giving way to a fluid mixture of 3/4 and 6/8 or to duple metre. Although the song is on a larger scale than the example by Cordier (No. 98), the melodic lines have an undeniably short-winded air in comparison with those of a later Dufay chanson such as *Adieu m'amour, adieu ma joye*. The presence of textless phrases in the vocal line has already been remarked in Cordier's *Se cuer d'amant*; they occur frequently in Dufay's chansons at all periods in his creative life.

TRANSLATIONS

Lovely lady, agree to keep me as your lover, for you are truly my only sweetheart. My heart strives to serve you, if it is your pleasure.
    On this New Year's Day I want to offer you this my heart, which can protect you from all grief and sadness.
    Lovely lady . . . sweetheart.
    You can make me languish, and rejoice, and be full of great joy. This is why my heart does not cease to beg and beseech you.
    Lovely lady . . . pleasure.

99. Belle, veullies moy retenir

Rondeau   Guillaume Dufay (*c*.1400–1474)

15 Contratenor: E for F   26 Contratenor: C for B   31 Contratenor: quaver C

100. Dueil angoisseus

Ballade Gilles Binchois (*c*.1400–1460)

Escorial, MS V III 24, ff. 36v–38r.

Regarded as one of the finest chanson composers of his generation, Binchois was employed at the Burgundian court from 1430 until his death. The master of an intimate and fairly small-scale idiom, he only rarely attempted the larger forms of the day, such as the cyclic mass and the motet. This example shows the essentials of his style – melodically direct, rhythmically uncomplicated, and with a distinctly 'modern' ear for euphonious chord progressions. As in many ballades, the repeated 'a' section is provided with those ouvert and clos endings which first appeared in the trobador-trouvère repertory some three hundred years earlier. The clos ending is re-used to finish the 'b' section. The

placing of a melisma over the penultimate syllable of a line of text was very common in the chanson for most of the 15th century. *Dueil angoisseus* was an extremely popular piece and was copied into many manuscripts; the Escorial source contains two other optional contratenor lines which are not printed here.

TRANSLATION
Grief fraught with anguish, uncontrolled passion, sorrow, despair full of madness, endless languor and ill-omened life filled with weeping, anguish, and torment, my heart is unhappy and lives on obscurely, my body wrapt in gloom and about to depart all the time and continually, if I cannot be cured or just die.

101. Verlangen thut mich krencken

Monophonic Lied   Anonymous (German, *c.*1450)

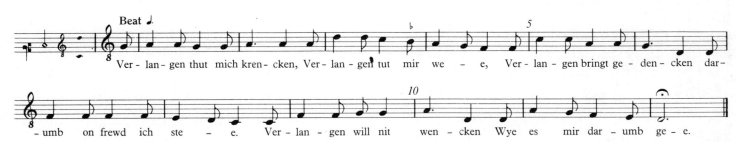

Berlin, Deutsche Bibliothek, MS 40613, f. 33.

The monophonic tradition survived in Germany for much longer than it did in other parts of Europe, being extant (albeit in a decadent state) as late as 1600. During the 15th century German composers took relatively slowly to polyphonic composition, and monophonic songs like this example continued to form the standard repertory in the Lieder manuscripts. The tradition of the Minnelied was virtually dead by 1400,

and it was supplanted by the twin genres of the *Meistergesang* (songs by an urbanized middle class and aristocracy, to serious, weighty texts) and the lighter, amorous Lied whose character is illustrated here. The text of only the first verse is given here.

TRANSLATION
Longing makes me love-sick, longing causes me pain, longing brings unhappy thoughts, because of that I am without joy. Longing will not yield, whatever happens to me.

102. Saint Thomas honour we

Carol   Anonymous (English, *c.*1430)

(Superius)
Saint Tho - mas ho - - - - nour___ we, thro whose blood Ho -

(Contratenor)

(Tenor)
Saint Tho - mas ho - - - - nour___ we, thro whose blood Ho -

- ly ___ Church ___ is ___ made ___ free.   1. All   Ho - ly
                                                 2. The   king   ex -
                                                 3. All   ben   ex -

- ly ___ Church ___ is ___ made ___ free.   1. All   Ho - ly
                                                 2. The   king   ex -
                                                 3. All   ben   ex -

Church___ was ___ but ___ a thrall,   all Ho - ly Church ___ was ___ but ___ a thrall,
- iled ___ him ___ out ___ of land,   the king ex - iled ___ him ___ out ___ of land,
- iled ___ that ___ to ___ him lang,   all ben ex - iled ___ that ___ to ___ him lang,

all Ho - ly Church ___ was but ___ a thrall,
the king ex - iled ___ him out of land,
all ben ex - iled ___ that to ___ him lang,

Church ___ was but a thrall,   all Ho - ly Church ___ was but a thrall,
- iled ___ him out of land,   the king ex - iled ___ him out of land,
- iled ___ that to him lang,   all ben ex - iled ___ that to him lang,

thro king and tem - po - ral ___ lor - dës ___ all, to he was ___ slain ___ in
and took his good ___ in his ___ hand, for - bid - ding ___ both ___ free
wo - men, chil - dren, ___ old ___ men a - - mong, young babes that ___ weep - ed ___

thro king and tem - po - ral lor - dës ___ all, to he was slain ___ in
and took his good ___ in ___ his ___ hand, for - bid - ding both ___ free
wo - men, chil - dren, ___ old men a - - mong, young babes that weep - - ed

Order of performance: Burden I, Verse 1, Burden II, Verse 2, Burden II, Verse 3, Burden II. The manuscript contains four more verses.

London, British Library, MS Egerton 3307, ff. 62v–63r.
J. Stevens, *Medieval Carols*, Musica Britannica, IV (London, R/1958), pp. 48–9.

The *carol* was an English poetic form consisting of a number of similarly-constructed stanzas and a separate unit called a *burden* which alternated with the stanzas. During the 14th century the Franciscans encouraged the writing of carols with religious texts, and by the beginning of the 15th century these were being set in polyphony. The texts of many polyphonic carols relate to the church festivals between

Christmas and Epiphany – the feasts of St Stephen, the Holy Innocents, St John, St Thomas of Canterbury, etc. – and it is probable that such pieces were sung as substitutes for the *Benedicamus Domino*. The probability is increased by the appearance of these words and/or the phrase *Deo gratias* in several of the texts. The polyphonic carol had two musical units – one for the burden and the other for the stanzas. The burden was sung first and then after every stanza. Sometimes, as in this example, there was a separate introductory burden which took the place of the first statement of the main burden and was not heard again. The alternation of passages in two and three parts is a feature of the genre.

103. Now wolde y fayne

Song   Anonymous (English, mid-15th century)

Oxford, Bodleian Library, MS Ashmole 191, f. 191r.

England was slow to develop a repertory of courtly polyphonic song equivalent to the Franco-Burgundian chanson. Most of the few compositions surviving from the first half of the 15th century are in two voices, and range from decidedly primitive pieces to quite polished settings like this example. Although *Now wolde y fayne* and No. 57 obviously inhabit quite different artistic worlds, it is interesting to note the persistence of the third as a basic interval in English two-part counterpoint.

104. *From* Fundamentum Organisandi

Organ treatise (*c*.1452–5)   **Conrad Paumann** (1409–73)

104a. Preambulum super fa

104b. Enavois

Berlin, Staatsbibliothek, Mus. MS 40613. No. 104a p. 92, No. 104b p. 70.

During the 15th century organ building, organ playing, and the composition of organ music became more highly developed in Germany than in any other part of Europe. German craftsmen devised the pedalboard, while German composers established an idiomatic style of keyboard figuration. The treatise *Fundamentum Organisandi* by the famed blind organist and composer Conrad Paumann was copied into the final pages of the 'Lochamer liederbuch', a source of mid-15th century German music. It contains two main types of composition. The first consists of preludes like example (a), in which the right hand superimposes rapid figuration over a simple foundation.

The second type of organ composition consists of settings of cantus firmi taken either from the plainsong repertory or from polyphonic pieces. As in example (b), the cantus firmus is usually given to the left hand in something like its original form, while the right hand plays a more lively counter-melody above it. In this case the cantus firmus is the tenor part of a chanson whose remaining text has not been preserved.

105. Falla con misuras (La Bassa Castiglia)

Basse danse Gulielmus (Italian, mid-15th century)

Perugia, Biblioteca Communale, MS 431, ff. 105v–106r

The *basse danse* was a popular courtly dance in France and the Low Countries (and in Italy under the title of *Bassadanza*) during the 15th and 16th centuries. The name probably derives from the low, gliding steps by which it was characterised. Basse danse melodies consist of monorhythmic cantus firmi, above and around which lively counterpoints would have been improvised by one or two instrumentalists (the favourite ensemble consisted of a slide trumpet playing the cantus firmus and two shawms providing the decoration). Many basse danse cantus firmi survive; each cantus firmus has its own choreography, indicated by a sequence of letters each of which stands for a certain step. Because they were usually improvised, polyphonic settings of basse danses have rarely come down to us. This example, which may date from about 1470, is one of the earliest polyphonic arrangements to have survived. The cantus firmus (a tune entitled *La Spagna*, of which some other settings are known) is in the lower part, and the upper stave has a florid counterpoint of a markedly improvisatory character. The basse danse was often paired with a following more lively dance called *pas de Brabant* (in Italy, *saltarello*). The Italians also cultivated an even more animated dance called *piva*, and a more stately *quaternaria* or *saltarello tedesco*.

106. Ingrata

Ballo **Anonymous (Italian, 15th century)**

F–Pn 972 10.

The nature of the Italian *ballo* was less stereotyped than that of the basse danse. Its music could be played or sung. Often it depicted in mime some action or event suggested by its title; in order to do so it freely alternated sections of melody moving at different speeds and in different rhythms. In this example the participants would probably have been two men and a woman – the 'ungrateful lady' of the title. The choreography of the dance would have depicted the advances of the suitors and her rejection of them.

Several Italian treatises on dance survive from the 15th century – *De arte saltandi* (Domenico da Piacenza, c. 1416), *L'arte della danza* (Antonio Cornazano, 1455), *De practica seu arte tripudii* (Guglielmo Ebreo, 1463). Their instructions are not always totally clear and unambiguous, however, and it did not seem possible to give a definitive choreography for this example.

Printed editions of compositions included in the Anthology

This list is selective, omitting publications whose editorial methods seemed to us to be seriously at variance with current scholarly practice. Where we have incorporated an existing edition into the anthology, an asterisk follows the number of the example. In all other cases we have prepared new editions for ourselves from the sources listed in the commentaries. Comparison of our editions with those in the following list will reveal numerous differences, many of which arise through our having chosen a different source as our main musical text. Brackets enclose the volume number (roman numerals) and page number (arabic numerals) of each printed edition.

H. Anglès, *Las Musica de las Cantigas de Santa Maria del Rey Alfonso el Sabio* (Barcelona, 1943): 28 (II, 37); 29 (II, 321).

W. Apel, *French Secular Music of the late Fourteenth Century* (Cambridge, Mass., 1950); 73 (108).

P. Aubry, *Cent Motets de XIII Siècle* (Paris, 1908): 44 (II, 163); 45 (II, 147); 46 (II, 159); 47 (II, 60).

M. Bent and A. Hughes, *The Old Hall Manuscript* (Rome, 1969): 66 (I, 259); 67 (I, 138).

H. Besseler, *Guillelmi Dufay Opera Omnia* (Rome, 1947–66): 89 (IV, 3); 99 (VI, 52).

C. van den Borren, *Missa Tornacensis* (Rome, 1957): 61 (1).

M. Bukofzer, *John Dunstable Complete Works* (London, R/1970): 97 (124).

P. Doe, *Sanctus, Magnificat* (Exeter, 1973): 64 (1).

F. Gennrich, *Lo Gai Saber: 50 Ausgewählte Troubadourlieder* (Darmstadt, 1959): 14 (15); 15 (49).

M. Gerbert, *Scriptores Ecclesiastici de Musica Sacra* (St Blaise, 1784): 37a (I, 164); 37b (I, 166); 37c (I, 167); 37d (I, 169); 37e (I, 170).

N. Greenberg and W. Smoldon, *The Play of Herod* (New York, 1965): 12 (1).

P. Gülke, *Johannes Pullois Opera Omnia* (Rome, 1967): 91 (3).

U. Günther, *The Motets of the Manuscripts Chantilly, Musée Condé, 564 (olim 1047) and Modena, Biblioteca Estense, α.M.5.24 (olim lat. 568)* (Rome, 1965): 59 (23).

A. Holschneider, *Die Organa von Winchester* (Hildesheim, 1968): 38* (163).

R. Hoppin, *The Cypriot–French Repertory of the Manuscript Torino, Biblioteca Nazionale, J. II. 9* (Rome, 1960–63): 60 (II, 34).

A. Hughes, see M. Bent above.

Liber Usualis (Tournai, 1963): 2* (742); 6* (147 and 782); 7* (254); 8* (375); 9* (561).

F. Liuzzi, *La Lauda e i Primordi della Musica Italiana* (Rome, 1935): 27 (II, 361).

N. Pirrotta, *Music of Fourteenth-Century Italy* (Rome, 1954–64): 74 (II, 36); 76 (IV, 1); 79 (III, 12).

D. Plamenac, *Keyboard Music of the Late Middle Ages in Codex Faenza 117* (Rome, 1972): 76 (80); 85 (80).

Polyphonic Music of the Fourteenth Century (various editors, including Leo Schrade and W. T. Marrocco, Monaco, 1956ff.): 58 (I, 76); 61 (I, 110); 62* (I, 162); 63 (XII, 17); 68 (III, 189); 69 (II, 2); 70 (III, 88); 71 (III, 150); 75 (VIII, 28); 76 (VI, 80); 77 (IV, 148); 78 (IV, 192); 79 (VII, 160); 80 (VIII, 117).

G. Prado, 'Mozarabic Melodies' in *Speculum* (1928): 3* (III, 235, 237).

G. Reaney, *Early Fifteenth-Century Music* (Rome, 1955–69): 98 (I, 8).

W. Rehm, *Die Chansons von Gilles Binchois* (Mainz, 1957): 100 (45).

H. Rietsch, *Gesange von Frauenlob, Reinmar von Zweter und Alexander* (Graz, 1960): 34 (67).

Y. Rokseth, *Polyphonies du XIII Siècle* (Paris, 1935–48): 45 (II, 42, 135); 46 (II, 174); 47 (II, 139); 52 (II, 1).

W. Schmieder, *Lieder von Neidhart (von Reuenthal)* (Graz, 1960): 32 (38).

W. Smoldon, see N. Greenberg, above.

H. Stäblein-Harder, *Fourteenth-Century Mass Music in France* (Rome, 1962): 62 (133).

D. Stevens, *Music in Honour of St Thomas of Canterbury* (London, 1970): 48 (20).

D. Stevens, *The Treasury of English Church Music* (London, 1965): 55 (I, 41).

J. Stevens, *Medieval Carols* (London, 1952): 102* (48).

E. Wellesz, *The Music of the Byzantine Church* (Cologne, 1959): 1* (53).

H. van der Werf, *The Chansons of the Troubadours and Trouvères* (Utrecht, 1972): 14* (93); 25 (124).

N. Wilkins, *The Lyric Works of Adam de la Halle* (Rome, 1967): 56 (56).